The ADHD Marketer

Turn Your Neurodiverse Mind into a Marketing Superpower

Richard Lowe

The Writing King

The ADHD Marketer: Turn Your Neurodiverse Mind into a Marketing Superpower

Table of Contents

See books by Richard Lowe at

https://masterofworlds.com

5

Get free publishing insights and industry updates at

https://thewritingking.substack.com

For ghostwriting and book coaching services see

https://thewritingking.com

Disclaimer

I'm not a doctor, therapist, psychologist, or any kind of medical professional. I'm a marketer with ADHD who figured out how to make marketing work for a brain like mine.

This isn't medical advice. Need help with mental health, medications, or getting diagnosed? Talk to real professionals. I can't help you there.

What I can help you with is marketing. I've spent years figuring out how to market myself, my services, and my books while dealing with ADHD, anxiety, and all the chaos that comes with a neurodivergent brain. This book is me sharing what worked.

Your results will vary. What works for me might flop for you. Take what's useful, toss the rest. You know your brain better than I do.

I'm not responsible if you try something from this book and it bombs, or if you make business decisions based on what I wrote. You're an adult. Make your own choices.

The marketing strategies here come from my experience and other neurodivergent marketers I know. They're real tactics from real people, not theory from textbooks. Use your judgment.

Preface

I wrote this book because I got sick of marketing advice that assumed I had a normal brain.

Every marketing book, course, and guru told me to "maintain consistent daily habits" and "network regularly" and "follow a systematic content calendar." Great advice if your brain works like a well-oiled machine. Terrible advice if your brain is more like a brilliant, chaotic fireworks show.

I have ADHD. I also have anxiety, some autistic traits, and I'm an introvert who ended up in marketing because when I left my corporate job I suddenly had to figure it out. For years, I tried forcing myself into the neurotypical marketing mold. I burned out repeatedly. I felt like a failure because I couldn't stick to the "proven systems" that worked for everyone else.

Then I stopped fighting my brain and started working with it.

Turns out my ADHD hyperfocus could help me dive deeper into research than most marketers ever do. My anxiety made me ridiculously good at spotting potential problems in campaigns before they launched. My introversion helped me build genuine one-on-one relationships with clients instead of superficial networking connections.

The problem wasn't my brain. The problem was trying to use someone else's operating system.

This book contains everything I wish someone had told me when I started marketing. No theory or psychology. Just practical solutions from someone who's been there. I've marketed myself as a freelancer, worked in agencies, run in-house marketing teams, and published books. I've done all of it with a neurodivergent brain, and I've figured out what works.

You don't need to fix your brain to be good at marketing. You need to learn how to use it properly.

Introduction

Marketing is not rocket science. But it can feel impossible when your brain works differently than everyone else's.

If you have ADHD, autism, anxiety, or you're an introvert, you've probably been told that marketing requires skills you don't have. You need to be naturally social. You need to love networking. You need to juggle multiple projects without losing focus. You need to handle rejection like it's no big deal.

That's all bullshit.

I've been marketing for over a decade with ADHD, anxiety, and introversion. I've built a successful ghostwriting and book coaching business, worked with major clients, and published books. I didn't do it by pretending to be neurotypical. I did it by figuring out how to make marketing work for the brain I have.

The marketing industry loves to talk about "best practices" and "proven systems." But most of these systems were designed by and for neurotypical brains. They assume you can maintain perfect consistency, handle constant social interaction, and switch between tasks smoothly. If you can't do these things, you're told you need to "work on yourself" or "develop better habits."

Here's what they don't tell you: your neurodivergent traits aren't bugs to fix. They're features to use.

Your ADHD hyperfocus can help you become an expert in your niche faster than anyone else. Your anxiety can make you ridiculously thorough at catching problems before they happen. Your autism can help you build systematic approaches that produce consistent results.

Your introversion can help you develop deeper relationships with clients and audiences.

The trick is learning how to use these traits strategically instead of fighting them constantly.

This book will show you how. It's organized around real problems you face as a neurodivergent marketer, with practical solutions that work. No theory, no fluff, no advice from people who've never had to figure out how to network when social interaction drains your battery.

Each chapter tackles a specific challenge: setting up your workspace so you can focus, managing projects when your brain jumps around, building relationships without burning out, creating content consistently without forcing fake productivity habits.

You'll also find strategies for different neurodivergent traits. If you have ADHD, there are chapters on using hyperfocus strategically and managing rejection sensitivity. If you're autistic, there are sections on using your systematic thinking and deep expertise. If you're an introvert, there are networking strategies that won't leave you exhausted.

What Actually Works for ADHD Marketers

If you have ADHD and you're trying to market anything, you've probably been told to create a content calendar, stick to a posting schedule, and maintain consistent daily habits. This advice comes from people who can do those things without their brain staging a revolt.

Here's the reality: your ADHD brain works differently and fighting it is exhausting. But when you learn to work with it instead of against it, you discover some serious advantages that neurotypical marketers don't have.

Your Hyperfocus Is Your Secret Weapon

Everyone talks about ADHD like it's all distraction and chaos. They ignore the hyperfocus part, which is your biggest marketing superpower.

When you hyperfocus on something, you can dive deeper into research, strategy, or content creation than most people ever will. You'll spend six hours straight learning everything about a client's industry or writing a comprehensive guide that covers angles your competitors missed entirely.

The key is learning how to trigger hyperfocus intentionally and protect it when it happens.

First, figure out what triggers your hyperfocus. For me, it's novelty and complexity. New industries, challenging problems, or research rabbit holes all get my brain locked in. For you, it might be visual content, data analysis, or writing. Pay attention to what grabs your brain and doesn't let go.

Second, clear your schedule when hyperfocus kicks in. This means having flexible deadlines and the ability to reschedule less important tasks. When your brain wants to spend eight hours creating the perfect campaign strategy, let it. You'll produce better work in those eight hours than you would in three weeks of forced productivity.

Third, protect your hyperfocus from interruptions. Turn off notifications, close your door, and tell people you're unavailable. Hyperfocus is fragile. One phone call or meeting can break it completely, and you might not get it back for days.

The biggest mistake ADHD marketers make is trying to force hyperfocus into neat little time blocks. You can't schedule it for Tuesday from 2-4 PM. You can only create conditions where it's more likely to happen and be ready to capitalize when it does.

Why Your Scattered Brain Sees Connections Others Miss

Your ADHD brain doesn't think in straight lines. It jumps around, makes weird connections, and sees patterns that more linear thinkers miss. This looks like a problem until you realize it's exactly what makes good marketing.

Marketing is about connecting ideas that don't obviously go together. Your scattered thinking style helps you see how a client's boring B2B software could appeal to creative professionals, or how a local restaurant could use the same strategy as a tech startup.

Normal brains think: "This is accounting software, so we should target accountants with features and benefits."

Your brain thinks: "This accounting software could save freelance designers hours of administrative work, which means more time for creative projects, which means we should show them getting back to what they love instead of talking about invoicing features."

The trick is learning to trust these connections instead of dismissing them as random thoughts.

When you have an idea that seems to come out of nowhere, write it down. Don't judge it, don't edit it, just capture it. Your brain is making connections in the background that you're not consciously aware of. Those random thoughts often turn into your best campaigns.

Keep an idea capture system that works for you. Some people use voice memos, others prefer quick notes in their phone. I use a simple text file that syncs across all my devices. The method doesn't matter as long as you can quickly dump ideas without interrupting your current task.

Review your captured ideas regularly. What seemed random in the moment often reveals patterns when you look at it later. You'll start to see themes and connections that turn into campaign concepts, content series, or positioning strategies.

The Three Things That Kill Your Productivity (And How to Fix Them)

ADHD marketers struggle with three productivity killers that traditional time management advice doesn't address: task switching costs, decision fatigue, and rejection sensitivity.

Task switching destroys your momentum. Every time you switch from writing to checking email to reviewing a design, your brain has to completely reorient itself. For ADHD brains, this transition takes longer and uses more mental energy than it does for neurotypical people.

The solution is batching similar tasks together. Instead of checking email throughout the day, check it twice: once in the morning and once in the afternoon. Instead of reviewing designs as they come in, set aside times for all your review work. Instead of writing a little bit on multiple projects, focus on one piece of content until it's finished.

Decision fatigue hits ADHD brains harder because we're already using extra mental energy to focus and filter distractions. By the end of the day, even simple decisions feel overwhelming.

Reduce decisions wherever possible. Create templates for common tasks like client onboarding, proposal writing, and content creation. Establish default responses for recurring situations. Use the same tools consistently instead of constantly evaluating new options.

I have email templates for probably 80% of the messages I send. I have proposal templates for different types of projects. I have content templates for different types of posts. This isn't about being lazy; it's about preserving mental energy for decisions that matter.

Rejection sensitivity makes marketing feel personally threatening. When a pitch gets ignored or a campaign underperforms, it feels like a judgment on you as a person rather than normal business feedback.

The solution is creating emotional distance through systems and processes. Instead of "my email campaign failed," it becomes "Email Campaign Test #47 had a 2.3% open rate, which suggests the subject line approach needs refinement."

Track everything as experiments rather than successes or failures. Keep detailed records so you can see patterns instead of fixating on individual results. Build feedback loops that focus on learning rather than judgment.

When a client gives critical feedback, resist the urge to defend or explain. Instead, ask questions to understand exactly what they want to see changed. Frame it as gathering data for your next iteration rather than personal criticism.

Your ADHD brain isn't broken. It's different. And different can be powerful in marketing if you learn how to use it strategically instead of constantly fighting it.

The rest of this book will show you how to build marketing systems that work with your neurodivergent traits instead of against them. But it starts with accepting that your brain is an asset, not a liability.

Hyperfocus Scheduling

Hyperfocus is your secret weapon, but most ADHD marketers waste it by fighting their natural rhythms or trying to force it into conventional time blocks. Traditional scheduling assumes you can maintain steady productivity throughout the day. Your brain works in intense bursts followed by recovery periods.

Stop trying to schedule hyperfocus and start preparing for it. You can't force hyperfocus to happen at 2 PM on Tuesday, but you can create conditions that make it more likely to occur and systems that capture its full value when it strikes.

Track your hyperfocus patterns for at least two weeks. Note what triggers deep focus sessions, what time of day they happen, how long they last, and what disrupts them. Look for patterns around sleep, caffeine, physical activity, and environmental factors.

My peak windows are 4 AM to 11 AM and 8 PM to midnight. Early morning before the world wakes up, and late evening after it quiets down again. Every productivity guru I've ever encountered has had an opinion about this. None of them were right about my brain. Your patterns will be different.

Protect potential hyperfocus windows by clearing external obligations. If you tend to hyperfocus on weekend mornings, don't schedule social activities or routine tasks during those times. Keep those windows available for when your brain wants to dive deep.

Create hyperfocus-ready workspaces with everything you need within reach. Research materials, note-taking tools, reference documents, snacks, water, and backup chargers should all be accessible without breaking concentration. Setup time kills hyperfocus momentum.

Build hyperfocus capture systems that preserve your work even when you can't complete projects in single sessions. Cloud-based documents, voice memos, quick note apps, and project folders help you resume work later without losing insights.

Use hyperfocus as your competitive advantage for complex projects. When other marketers are doing surface-level research, you're diving deep into customer psychology, competitive analysis, or industry trends. Your depth creates insights that drive better strategies.

Don't fight hyperfocus when it emerges, even if it's inconvenient timing. Cancel non-critical meetings, delegate routine tasks, and let yourself follow the energy. You'll produce more valuable work in four hours of hyperfocus than in two weeks of forced productivity.

Create transition rituals that help you shift from hyperfocus back to regular tasks. Deep focus sessions can leave you mentally depleted. Build in recovery time and gentle activities that help your brain return to baseline without crashing.

Using Urgency as Fuel

ADHD brains are motivated by urgency in ways that neurotypical brains aren't. Deadlines that stress other people improve your focus and creativity. The adrenaline and time pressure help override distractibility and analysis paralysis.

Instead of fighting your urgency orientation, design work systems that use it productively. This doesn't mean procrastinating until the last minute on everything, but it does mean understanding how urgency improves your performance.

Create artificial urgency for projects that lack natural deadlines. Set shorter internal deadlines for long-term projects, use timer-based work sessions, or establish accountability partnerships that create external pressure.

Break large projects into urgent micro-deadlines rather than distant final deadlines. "Complete competitor analysis by Friday" feels urgent. "Complete marketing strategy by next month" doesn't generate the same focus-enhancing pressure.

Use urgency to overcome perfectionism and analysis paralysis. When time pressure forces quick decisions, you stop overthinking and start executing. Set "good enough" deadlines that prevent endless revision cycles.

Schedule urgent work during your highest-energy periods. If urgency helps you focus, combine it with times when your brain is more alert and creative. This amplifies both the energy boost and the urgency benefit.

Build urgency into client projects through phased deliverables and regular check-ins. Instead of one final deadline six weeks away, create weekly milestones with deliverables. This maintains urgency throughout the project timeline.

Use competition and gamification to create urgency around routine tasks. Challenge yourself to complete email responses in 20 minutes, see how many social media posts you can create in an hour, or race against previous completion times.

Batch urgent tasks together to maximize the focus benefits. When you're in urgency mode, complete multiple deadline-driven tasks in the same session. The momentum carries over between related activities.

Creative Brainstorming That Produces Results

Traditional brainstorming doesn't work for ADHD brains. The "no criticism" rule encourages the scattered thinking that already challenges your executive function. Open-ended ideation without structure leads to idea overload rather than workable concepts.

ADHD-friendly brainstorming combines structure with creative freedom. You need frameworks that channel your associative thinking productively while preventing idea overwhelm.

Use constraint-based brainstorming instead of open ideation. Give your brain boundaries to work within: "Generate 10 email subject lines for busy executives" works better than "brainstorm email ideas." Constraints focus your creativity rather than limiting it.

Try rapid-fire ideation with strict time limits. Set a timer for 10-15 minutes and generate as many ideas as possible without editing or evaluating. The time pressure prevents overthinking and taps into your brain's quick-association abilities.

Build on ideas immediately rather than collecting lists for later evaluation. When you generate an interesting concept, spend 5-10 minutes developing it before moving to the next idea. This captures your creative momentum while it's active.

Use visual brainstorming methods that engage your spatial thinking. Mind maps, concept clusters, or image boards help your brain make connections that text-based brainstorming might miss.

Combine research with ideation rather than treating them as separate phases. Your ADHD brain often generates best ideas while gathering information. Research competitor approaches, customer feedback, or industry trends, then let ideas emerge from the data.

Create idea evaluation frameworks that help you choose workable concepts quickly. Rate ideas on implementation difficulty, potential impact, and resource requirements. This prevents you from falling in love with brilliant but impractical concepts.

Use your hyperfocus periods for deep creative work rather than surface-level brainstorming. When your brain is locked into creative mode, develop comprehensive campaigns, detailed strategies, or complex content series rather than just generating quick ideas.

Test ideas quickly rather than perfecting them mentally. Your ADHD brain can see so many possibilities that you get stuck in analysis mode. Build simple prototypes, create rough drafts, or run small experiments to get real feedback.

Document everything immediately because ADHD brains are terrible at remembering ideas later. Use voice memos, quick notes, or photos to capture concepts when they emerge. Great ideas that aren't recorded are worthless ideas.

Your ADHD traits aren't obstacles to overcome in marketing - they're advantages to use strategically. When you work with your brain instead of against it, you can outthink, outpace, and out-create marketers who rely on conventional approaches.

If You're Autistic and Marketing

Marketing feels like it was designed to torture autistic people. You're supposed to be naturally charismatic, love spontaneous conversations, and constantly adapt to changing trends. You're expected to network at loud events, make small talk with strangers, and pivot strategies on a whim.

But here's what the marketing industry doesn't understand: your autistic traits aren't obstacles to overcome. They're competitive advantages that most marketers would kill for.

Your Obsessive Research Is Gold

When you get interested in something, you don't just learn about it. You become an expert. You read everything, analyze patterns, and understand connections that surface-level researchers miss completely.

This obsessive research style is exactly what great marketing requires, but most marketers are too impatient to do it properly.

While your competitors are skimming blog posts and copying what everyone else is doing, you're diving deep into industry reports, academic studies, and obscure forums where your target audience hangs out. You understand the nuances that others miss.

When I worked with a client in the manufacturing industry, most marketers would have read a few trade publications and called it research. But my autistic hyperfocus kicked in, and I spent weeks understanding the entire supply chain, regulatory environment, and technical specifications that mattered to their customers.

That research uncovered positioning opportunities that no one else saw. While competitors were talking about generic benefits like "efficiency" and "cost savings," we could speak directly to pain points like "reducing changeover time for multi-SKU production runs" and "maintaining FDA compliance during equipment transitions."

The key is learning how to channel your research obsession strategically instead of getting lost in interesting but irrelevant rabbit holes.

Set research boundaries before you start. Decide what questions you need to answer and what level of detail is sufficient. Write these down so you can refer back when you start going too deep.

Use your special interests as research advantages. If you're obsessed with a particular industry, technology, or topic, look for clients in that space. Your natural curiosity will drive better research than forced interest ever could.

Document everything as you research. Your brain notices patterns and connections that you might not consciously recognize in the moment. Keep detailed notes so you can review and synthesize later.

Don't apologize for being thorough. Clients might be surprised by the depth of your research, but they'll appreciate the insights that come from it. Most marketers give them surface-level strategies. You give them deep understanding.

How to Turn Your Need for Systems Into Client Value

You probably have systems for everything. How you organize your files, process information, manage projects, and make decisions. Other people might see this as rigid or obsessive. Smart clients see it as valuable.

Your systematic approach means you catch details that other marketers miss, you follow processes consistently, and you deliver predictable results. In an industry full of creative chaos, this is a huge competitive advantage.

But you need to learn how to sell your systems as features, not hide them as quirks.

Create documented processes for everything you do. Client onboarding, campaign development, content creation, performance analysis. Having these systems written down shows clients exactly what they're getting and builds confidence in your approach.

Show clients your systems during the sales process. Walk them through your research methodology, planning framework, and quality control processes. This differentiates you from marketers who wing it and hope for the best.

Use your systems to set clear expectations. When clients understand your process, they know when to provide input, what deliverables to expect, and how timeline changes affect the overall project.

Build flexibility into your systems. This might feel contradictory, but rigid systems break when clients change their minds or market conditions shift. Build decision points and alternative paths into your processes.

I have a content strategy framework that includes 15 different research inputs, 7 strategic positioning options, and 4 different content calendar approaches. Clients don't need to understand all the options, but having them documented means I can adapt systematically instead of starting from scratch.

Your systematic approach also helps with scope creep, which destroys profitability for many marketers. When you have documented processes, it's easy to identify when a client request falls outside the agreed scope.

Instead of saying "that feels like extra work," you can say "that request would require us to add the competitive positioning analysis module to our research phase, which takes an additional 8-12 hours."

Making Small Talk Optional (Networking Hacks)

Traditional networking advice assumes you enjoy small talk, can read social cues effortlessly, and thrive in noisy, crowded environments. If you're autistic, this advice is useless at best and torture at worst.

But networking isn't about small talk. It's about building professional relationships with people who can help your business. You can do this without pretending to enjoy cocktail party conversations.

Focus on one-on-one connections instead of group networking events. Schedule coffee meetings, phone calls, or video chats with people you want to know better. This eliminates the social complexity of group dynamics and lets you have deeper, more meaningful conversations.

Use your special interests as networking tools. If you're obsessed with data analysis, content strategy, or marketing automation, find communities where people discuss these topics. Join forums, Slack groups, or professional associations focused on your interests.

Prepare conversation frameworks ahead of time. Having a mental script reduces social anxiety and ensures you cover important topics. Prepare questions about their business challenges, current projects, and industry trends.

My standard networking conversation framework includes: How did you get into marketing? What's the biggest challenge in your current role? What trends are you paying attention to? What resources do you recommend? This gives me 30-45 minutes of natural conversation without needing to improvise.

Use online networking platforms. LinkedIn, Twitter, and industry platforms let you build relationships without face-to-face interaction. You can take time to craft thoughtful responses instead of thinking on your feet.

Follow up systematically. After meeting someone, send a LinkedIn connection request with a personal note referencing your conversation. Add them to your CRM or contact management system. Set reminders to check in periodically.

Attend structured networking events instead of unstructured social mixers. Industry conferences with educational sessions, workshops with learning objectives, or professional meetups with topics give you natural conversation starters and clear reasons to attend.

Bring a colleague or friend to networking events. Having someone you know eliminates the stress of walking into a room full of strangers. You can introduce each other and have someone to talk to between conversations.

Set realistic networking goals. Instead of "meet lots of people," aim for "have three meaningful conversations" or "learn about two new industry trends." Quality matters more than quantity.

Deep Expertise as Your Brand

Autistic people develop deep expertise in areas that interest them. While other marketers stay at surface level across many topics, you dive deep into subjects that fascinate you. This depth is valuable in marketing, where genuine expertise sets you apart from generic advice givers.

Your interests can become your professional brand when you connect them strategically to marketing applications. Instead of hiding your obsessions, use them as the foundation for thought leadership and business development.

Map your interests to marketing opportunities. If you're fascinated by data analysis, position yourself as the go-to expert for marketing analytics and conversion optimization. If you love studying consumer psychology, build your reputation around behavioral marketing and persuasion strategies.

My obsession with email marketing automation turned into my primary business focus. While other marketers treated email as just another channel, I spent years studying deliverability, segmentation psychology, and automation workflows. This depth created opportunities that surface-level knowledge never could.

Document your learning process as content that demonstrates your expertise. When you're researching your interests anyway, capture insights that others would find valuable. Turn your deep dives into blog posts, case studies, or educational resources.

Create comprehensive resources around your areas of expertise rather than quick tips and generic advice. Your natural tendency toward thoroughness produces guides, frameworks, and reference materials that become go-to resources in your field.

Use your systematic approach to expertise development as a competitive advantage. While others jump between trending topics, you build deep knowledge that compounds over time. This consistency creates authority that superficial knowledge can't match.

Connect your knowledge to broader business outcomes. Show how your deep understanding of email deliverability improves ROI, how your expertise in accessibility creates better user experiences, or how your knowledge of data privacy builds customer trust.

Position yourself as the specialist rather than trying to be a generalist. Clients will pay premium rates for deep expertise in areas they care about. Being the best email marketing expert in your region is more valuable than being a decent generalist marketer.

Build communities around your areas of expertise. Host discussions, create educational content, and connect with others who share your interests. These communities become referral sources and professional networks based on genuine shared interests.

Systematic Optimization

Your autistic brain excels at identifying patterns, creating systems, and optimizing processes for better results. While other marketers rely on intuition and best practices, you can build systematic approaches that consistently improve performance.

Turn your natural systematic thinking into documented processes that create competitive advantages. Your tendency to analyze and optimize everything becomes a business asset when applied strategically to marketing challenges.

Create detailed testing frameworks for campaign optimization. Instead of random A/B tests, develop systematic approaches that test one variable at a time, document results comprehensively, and build knowledge that informs future decisions.

My testing system includes hypothesis formation, statistical significance calculations, results documentation, and learning integration. This systematic approach produces more reliable insights than ad hoc testing ever could.

Build optimization systems around your areas of focus. If you specialize in email marketing, create systematic approaches to subject line testing, send time optimization, and segmentation refinement. If you focus on content marketing, develop systematic methods for topic research, performance analysis, and content improvement.

Use your attention to detail to identify optimization opportunities others miss. Small improvements in conversion rates, email deliverability, or page load speeds can have business impact when applied systematically across large campaigns.

Document your optimization processes so they can be repeated and improved over time. Create checklists, templates, and workflows that ensure consistent execution of your systematic approaches. This documentation also helps you explain your methods to clients and team members.

Apply systematic thinking to business development and client management. Create structured approaches for lead qualification, proposal development, and project management that reduce uncertainty and improve outcomes.

Use data systematically rather than relying on gut feelings or industry conventional wisdom. Track metrics consistently, analyze patterns over time, and make decisions based on evidence rather than assumptions.

Build feedback loops into your systems that enable continuous improvement. Regular performance reviews, client feedback collection, and process refinement ensure your systematic approaches evolve and improve over time.

Quality Assurance Systems

Your natural attention to detail and systematic thinking create quality assurance capabilities. While other marketers rush to launch campaigns, you catch the errors, inconsistencies, and problems that can destroy campaign effectiveness.

Turn your perfectionist tendencies into quality control systems that prevent expensive mistakes and ensure professional delivery. Your ability to spot details others miss becomes a valuable service that clients will pay premium rates for.

Create comprehensive quality checklists for different types of marketing deliverables. Email campaigns, website launches, social media content, and advertising campaigns all have potential failure points that systematic review processes can catch.

My email campaign checklist includes subject line testing, link verification, mobile rendering checks, segmentation accuracy, personalization functionality, unsubscribe link testing, and compliance verification. This systematic review prevents the errors that damage deliverability and campaign performance.

Build quality review processes into project timelines rather than treating them as optional final steps. Quality assurance requires time and attention, so schedule it appropriately rather than rushing through reviews under deadline pressure.

Develop quality standards that go beyond basic functionality to include brand consistency, user experience, and business objective alignment. Your systematic thinking helps you evaluate campaigns against multiple criteria rather than just checking for obvious errors.

Use your pattern recognition abilities to identify quality issues that aren't covered by standard checklists. Your brain notices inconsistencies in design, messaging, or user experience that others might miss.

Create quality documentation that helps others understand and maintain your standards. This includes style guides, brand guidelines, process documentation, and training materials that ensure quality standards persist even when you're not involved.

Apply quality thinking to client communication and project management. Systematic approaches to feedback collection, revision tracking, and approval processes prevent miscommunication and scope creep that can derail projects.

Build quality metrics into campaign performance tracking. Monitor not just conversion rates and engagement, but also error rates, consistency scores, and user experience indicators that reflect the quality of campaign execution.

Position your quality focus as a premium service rather than basic expectation. Clients who have worked with careless marketers will pay extra for someone who catches problems before they become expensive mistakes.

Use your quality systems to build long-term client relationships. Consistent, high-quality delivery creates trust and reduces client anxiety about working with you. This reliability leads to repeat business and referrals.

Autistic traits in marketing aren't obstacles to overcome - they're competitive advantages that create better results for clients and more sustainable businesses for you. Your systematic thinking, deep expertise, and quality focus are what the marketing industry needs more of.

Introverts in Loud Marketing Spaces

Marketing is supposed to be an extrovert's game. You're expected to love networking events, thrive on constant collaboration, and get energized by brainstorming sessions with the whole team. The industry celebrates the loud voices, the people who dominate meetings, and those who can work a room at conferences.

If you're an introvert, this probably makes you want to hide under your desk.

But introversion isn't a weakness in marketing. It's a different operating system that comes with serious advantages once you learn how to use it properly. You don't need to become an extrovert to succeed. You need to build systems that work with your energy patterns instead of against them.

Energy Budgeting That Works

Your energy is finite. Social interactions, meetings, brainstorming sessions, and networking events all drain your battery. Most introverts try to push through this and end up burned out, resentful, or performing poorly when their energy runs out.

Energy budgeting means treating your social energy like money in a bank account. You have a daily allowance, and you need to spend it strategically on the interactions that matter most.

Track your energy patterns for a week. Note what activities drain you, what gives you energy back, and how long you need to recover from high-drain situations. This becomes your baseline for planning.

I discovered that client calls drain me much more than internal team meetings. Conference calls are worse than in-person meetings. Networking events require a full day of recovery time. Knowing this helps me schedule strategically instead of randomly.

Plan your high-energy activities for when you're most charged. If you're a morning person, schedule important client calls early. If you hit your stride in the afternoon, protect that time for complex strategic work.

Build buffer time around draining activities. Don't schedule a networking event and a client presentation on the same day. Give yourself space to recharge between energy-intensive tasks.

Learn to say no to optional social activities that don't advance your goals. You don't need to attend every team happy hour, industry mixer, or casual coffee meeting. Your time and energy are valuable resources.

Create energy-giving rituals that help you recharge. This might be 15 minutes of quiet time between meetings, a walk around the block, or listening to music with headphones. Figure out what restores your energy and build it into your schedule.

Use asynchronous communication whenever possible. Email, Slack messages, and recorded videos let you communicate thoughtfully without the energy drain of real-time conversation. You can craft better responses when you have time to think.

Batch your social interactions. Instead of having meetings scattered throughout the day, cluster them together. This creates longer uninterrupted work periods and reduces the number of times you need to shift into social mode.

Set boundaries around your recharge time. Block time on your calendar for deep work, and treat it as seriously as any client meeting. Turn off notifications, close your door, and let people know you're unavailable.

One-to-One Relationship Building (Your Superpower)

Introverts often think they're bad at networking because they hate working a room full of strangers. But networking isn't about collecting business cards from 50 people at a cocktail party. It's about building meaningful professional relationships.

One-on-one conversations are where introverts shine. You're naturally better at deep conversations, active listening, and creating genuine connections. These skills are valuable in marketing, where authentic relationships drive business results.

Focus on quality over quantity. Instead of trying to meet everyone at an industry event, aim to have three meaningful conversations. Instead of maintaining superficial connections with hundreds of LinkedIn contacts, build deeper relationships with 20-30 key people.

Use your listening skills as a competitive advantage. Most people in marketing love to talk about themselves, their ideas, and their successes. If you can ask good questions and listen to the answers, you'll stand out immediately.

Prepare conversation starters that feel natural to you. Instead of generic small talk, ask about challenges in their industry, interesting projects they're working on, or resources they'd recommend. This leads to more substantive conversations that you'll enjoy.

Use coffee meetings and lunch conversations. These one-on-one formats play to your strengths and let you build relationships without the chaos of group networking. Most people are flattered when you ask to learn more about their work.

Follow up consistently but not aggressively. Send a thoughtful LinkedIn message referencing something from your conversation. Share an article that relates to their challenges. Make introductions when you meet someone who could help them.

Build relationships before you need them. Don't only reach out when you're looking for work or trying to sell something. Maintain regular contact by sharing useful information, congratulating them on achievements, or simply checking in.

Use your natural tendency toward deep thinking to provide value in relationships. When someone shares a challenge, you can think through potential solutions and follow up with thoughtful suggestions. This builds your reputation as someone worth knowing.

Create systems for relationship maintenance. Keep notes on important conversations, set reminders to check in with key contacts, and track how you can help people in your network. This systematic approach ensures you don't let valuable relationships fade.

Surviving Conferences Without Dying

Conferences are designed for extroverts. Loud environments, constant social interaction, packed schedules, and networking events that feel like cocktail parties. For introverts, they can be overwhelming to the point of being counterproductive.

But conferences are also where industry connections happen, where you learn about new trends, and where opportunities emerge. You can't avoid them entirely, but you can approach them strategically.

Choose your conferences carefully. Don't attend every industry event just because you're supposed to. Pick 2-3 conferences per year that align with your goals and offer the best potential return on your energy investment.

Plan your conference schedule with energy management in mind. Don't try to attend every session, networking event, and social gathering. Choose the most valuable activities and leave space for recharging.

Book accommodations that give you a refuge. A quiet hotel room where you can escape the chaos is essential. Consider staying an extra night so you can recover before returning to normal work.

Arrive early to get oriented before the crowds arrive. Scope out quiet spaces where you can retreat when you need a break. Identify less crowded areas for conversations. Plan your routes between sessions.

Use meal times strategically. Instead of attending large networking lunches, schedule one-on-one meals with people you want to connect with. This turns necessary eating time into valuable relationship building.

Prepare your introduction and conversation topics ahead of time. Having a mental script reduces the cognitive load of social interaction and ensures you communicate your value clearly even when you're drained.

Set realistic networking goals. Instead of "meet as many people as possible," aim for "have five meaningful conversations" or "connect with three potential collaborators." Quality beats quantity every time.

Take breaks regularly. Step outside for fresh air, find a quiet corner to check email, or retreat to your hotel room between sessions. Don't push through until you're completely depleted.

Follow up immediately after the conference while conversations are fresh in your mind. Send LinkedIn connections, share promised resources, and schedule follow-up calls. This is where introverts often excel because you're more thoughtful about follow-through.

Consider alternative networking approaches. Skip the official networking events and suggest coffee meetings with people. Host a small dinner for 6-8 people instead of working the main reception. Create intimate gatherings that play to your strengths.

Your introversion isn't a marketing disability. It's a different approach that can be effective when you understand how to use it. Introverted marketers often build stronger client relationships, create more thoughtful strategies, and produce higher quality work because they take time to think before acting.

The key is designing your marketing career around your energy patterns instead of fighting them. Build systems that protect your energy, focus on relationship quality over quantity, and create space for the deep thinking that produces your best work.

Thoughtful vs Fast Responses

The marketing world values quick responses and rapid-fire idea generation. Clients expect immediate email replies. Teams want instant feedback on proposals. Brainstorming sessions favor people who can think out loud quickly.

But thoughtful responses are often better than fast responses. Your natural tendency to process information before speaking can produce more insightful, strategic, and valuable contributions when positioned appropriately.

Establish response time expectations that work with your processing style. Instead of feeling pressured to reply immediately, set clear timelines that give you space to think while meeting client needs.

"I review emails twice daily and respond within 24 hours for non-urgent matters" sets appropriate expectations while giving you processing time. Most marketing communications aren't urgent despite feeling that way.

Use your preparation time as a competitive advantage in meetings and presentations. While others wing it, you come prepared with research, analysis, and thoughtful questions. This preparation often leads to better discussions and stronger outcomes.

Develop frameworks for common situations that let you respond thoughtfully without taking excessive time. Email templates, meeting agendas, and project checklists help you maintain quality while improving response speed.

Ask for time to consider complex requests rather than giving immediate responses you might later regret. "Let me think about this and get back to you by tomorrow" is often better than a hasty decision made under pressure.

Use written communication to showcase your thoughtful analysis. Your carefully crafted emails, detailed project proposals, and comprehensive reports often impress clients more than verbal presentations.

Build thinking time into your process for important decisions. Schedule time for analysis, research additional information if needed, and consider multiple perspectives before committing to strategies or recommendations.

Position your thoughtful approach as thorough analysis rather than slow decision-making. "I like to research all the options before making recommendations" sounds strategic, not indecisive.

Public Speaking Without Panic

Public speaking terrifies many introverts, but it's often necessary for marketing success. Conference presentations, client pitches, webinars, and team meetings all require speaking to groups. The key is reducing the energy drain while maintaining effective communication.

Prepare extensively to reduce anxiety and cognitive load during presentations. Know your material so well that you can focus on delivery rather than trying to remember content. This preparation also builds confidence that reduces speaking anxiety.

Create detailed presentation outlines with key talking points, transition phrases, and backup information. Having structure reduces the improvisation that many introverts find stressful in speaking situations.

Practice presentations multiple times before important speaking engagements. Rehearsal helps you identify potential problems, smooth out transitions, and build familiarity that reduces performance anxiety.

Use slides and visual aids to guide your presentation and provide talking points. Well-designed slides help you stay on track while giving the audience visual information that supports your verbal content.

Start with smaller speaking opportunities to build confidence before tackling major presentations. Team meetings, informal client calls, or small group workshops provide practice without high-stakes pressure.

Focus on delivering value rather than entertaining the audience. Your goal is sharing useful information, not being charismatic or funny. This shift in focus reduces performance pressure and plays to your strengths.

Arrive early to speaking venues to get comfortable with the space and technology. Familiarity with the environment reduces anxiety and helps you feel more in control during the presentation.

Build recovery time into your schedule after major speaking engagements. Public speaking is draining for introverts, so plan quiet time to recharge after presentations.

Use storytelling and case studies to make presentations more engaging without requiring high energy. Well-prepared stories feel more natural than improvised content and help you connect with audiences.

Consider alternative presentation formats that feel more comfortable. Webinars, recorded videos, or panel discussions might feel less intimidating than solo presentations to large groups.

Remember that many audience members prefer thoughtful, well-prepared presentations over high-energy performances. Your natural speaking style may resonate better with decision-makers than flashy presentation techniques.

Introvert marketing strategies aren't about becoming more extroverted. They're about designing your marketing practice around your natural strengths while managing the energy costs of necessary social activities.

Your thoughtful approach to communication, preparation-focused work style, and preference for deep relationships over superficial networking can become competitive advantages when used strategically.

The Anxiety/Perfectionist Marketer

If you have anxiety or perfectionist tendencies, marketing feels like a minefield. You're supposed to move fast, test things, and be okay with failure. You're expected to publish content that's "good enough," launch campaigns before they're perfect, and iterate based on results.

This goes against every instinct you have.

Your anxiety tells you that one bad campaign could ruin your reputation. Your perfectionism insists that everything needs to be flawless before anyone sees it. Your brain conjures up worst-case scenarios for every decision and finds flaws in every strategy.

But here's what most people don't understand: anxiety and perfectionism can be powerful assets in marketing when you learn to channel them properly. The trick is knowing when to listen to these tendencies and when to override them.

When Perfectionism Helps (Quality Control)

Perfectionism gets a bad rap, but it's a competitive advantage in several key areas of marketing. Your obsessive attention to detail catches mistakes that other marketers miss. Your high standards produce work that stands out in a sea of mediocrity.

The key is learning where perfectionism adds value versus where it creates paralysis.

Perfectionism is gold for quality control. You spot typos, broken links, design inconsistencies, and logical gaps that others miss. This attention to detail prevents embarrassing mistakes and builds client confidence in your work.

Use your perfectionist tendencies for final reviews and client-facing deliverables. Campaign strategies, proposals, and important emails should get your full perfectionist treatment. These are the moments where quality matters.

Your perfectionism also helps with brand consistency. You notice when fonts don't match, when messaging is inconsistent across channels, or when visual elements don't align properly. This creates a more professional brand experience that clients and customers notice subconsciously.

Research and data analysis benefit from perfectionist attention to detail. You're more likely to verify sources, double-check calculations, and catch statistical errors that could lead to wrong conclusions. This thoroughness produces better strategic insights.

Client communication is another area where perfectionism pays off. Your carefully crafted emails are clearer, more professional, and less likely to be misunderstood than hastily written messages. This reduces back-and-forth confusion and builds stronger relationships.

Legal and compliance issues are where perfectionism can save you. You're more likely to read the fine print, follow platform guidelines, and ensure campaigns meet regulatory requirements. One missed compliance issue can be costly.

The perfectionist's obsession with preparation also helps with presentations and pitches. You anticipate questions, prepare backup slides, and rehearse until you're confident. This preparation shows and increases your win rate.

When It Kills You (Everything Else)

Perfectionism becomes destructive when it prevents you from taking action, testing ideas, or learning from real market feedback. If you're spending weeks perfecting a social media post or months refining a strategy before launching, perfectionism is hurting your results.

Content creation is where perfectionism often becomes paralyzing. You write and rewrite blog posts until they're theoretical masterpieces but never publish them. You create social media content that's perfectly crafted but posted so infrequently that nobody notices.

The solution is setting "good enough" standards for regular content. Your weekly blog post doesn't need to be award-winning. Your daily social media posts don't need to be perfect. They need to be consistent and valuable.

Campaign testing suffers under perfectionism because you want to control all variables before launching. But marketing is messy. The best insights come from real market feedback, not perfect theoretical planning.

Launch imperfect campaigns with clear success metrics and iteration plans. A campaign that's 80% ready and launched this month will produce better results than a campaign that's 100% perfect and launched next quarter.

Email marketing is another area where perfectionism kills momentum. You obsess over subject lines, rewrite copy endlessly, and delay sending until everything is perfect. Meanwhile, your competitors are sending regular emails and building relationships with your potential customers.

Set time limits for email creation. Give yourself 2 hours to write and send a newsletter. The deadline forces you to make decisions and move forward instead of endlessly tweaking.

Perfectionism also destroys experimentation and learning. You want to know the "right" answer before testing anything. But marketing is about discovering what works through systematic testing, not theoretical perfection.

Embrace "good enough" experiments. Run quick tests with limited budgets to gather data. You're not looking for perfect results; you're looking for directional insights that inform your next iteration.

Social media perfectionism is destructive because these platforms reward consistency over perfection. A stream of good posts beats an occasional perfect post every time.

Batch content creation and set publication schedules. Create a week's worth of social media content in one session, schedule it, and resist the urge to constantly revise before it goes live.

5-Minute Fixes for Analysis Paralysis

Analysis paralysis happens when your anxiety about making the wrong decision prevents you from making any decision at all. You research endlessly, consider every possible outcome, and delay action while looking for the perfect solution.

Here are quick techniques to break the paralysis cycle:

Set decision deadlines. Give yourself a timeframe to make a decision, then stick to it. "I will choose an email marketing platform by Friday at 5 PM." When the deadline arrives, pick the best option based on available information.

Decide with incomplete information. You will never have all the data you want. Waiting for certainty is just procrastination with better branding. Pick a threshold — say, enough information to make a defensible case — and commit when you hit it.

Sort decisions by how reversible they are. Email subject lines, social media timing, ad copy — these can all be changed in ten minutes if they're wrong. Don't spend an hour on something you can fix in seconds. Save your decision energy for things that actually stick.

Ask yourself which option you'd regret not trying. Not what sounds safer, not what looks better on paper — what would you wish you'd done? That question cuts through analysis faster than any framework.

Set a hard stop on research. Pick a time, gather everything you can find before it, then decide. The research loop never closes on its own. You have to close it.

Default to experiments over decisions. Instead of committing to the perfect long-term solution, run a 30-day test. Takes the pressure off permanent choices and gives you real data.

Build decision criteria before you need them. When you're calm, establish what matters: budget, fit, integration requirements. Then when you're overwhelmed and need to choose, you're just checking boxes instead of thinking from scratch.

Flip a coin when you're stuck between two options. Not because the coin decides — but because the moment it lands, you'll know whether you're relieved or disappointed. That reaction tells you what you actually wanted.

Stop looking for the best option. Look for the first option that's good enough and move. Maximizing is for people with unlimited time. You don't have that.

Pre-decide your stuck moves. When you can't choose between two campaign ideas, test both with small budgets. When you can't pick a blog topic, write about the last question a client asked you. Remove the decision from the paralysis moment by making it before you get there.

Your anxiety and perfectionism aren't character flaws to overcome. They're psychological patterns that can be channeled productively. Use your perfectionist attention to detail where quality matters most. Use your anxiety as an early warning system for potential problems. But don't let either prevent you from taking action and learning from real market feedback.

Deadline Pressure Management

Anxiety around deadlines can either motivate peak performance or create paralysis that makes deadlines impossible to meet. Learning to work with deadline pressure rather than being overwhelmed by it turns time constraints into productivity tools.

Most deadline anxiety comes from uncertainty about whether you can complete quality work in the available time. Reducing this uncertainty through better planning and realistic scope management decreases anxiety while improving outcomes.

Break large projects into smaller milestones with individual deadlines rather than focusing on final delivery dates. "Complete research phase by Monday, finish first draft by Wednesday, finalize copy by Friday" feels more manageable than "deliver campaign by Friday."

Build buffer time into all project timelines to account for perfectionist tendencies and unexpected complications. If you estimate a project will take 10 hours, schedule 15 hours. This buffer reduces deadline pressure while ensuring quality standards.

Create "good enough" definitions for different deadline scenarios. When time is unlimited, you might revise content five times. When deadlines are tight, define what constitutes acceptable quality that meets client needs without perfectionist polish.

Use time pressure as a tool to overcome analysis paralysis and perfectionist procrastination. Setting artificial deadlines for decision-making forces you to move forward instead of endlessly researching or revising.

Develop emergency protocols for when deadlines become impossible to meet. Have frameworks for communicating with clients about timeline changes, strategies for reducing project scope, and backup plans for delivering partial work.

Track your time estimation accuracy to improve future planning. If you consistently underestimate how long tasks take, adjust your planning accordingly. If you overestimate, you can take on more work or improve your processes.

Practice working under time pressure in low-stakes situations to build confidence for important deadlines. Set artificial time constraints for routine tasks to develop comfort with deadline pressure.

Dealing with Imposter Syndrome

The problem with the phrase "imposter syndrome" is that it implies the feeling is wrong. Sometimes it's not. Sometimes you genuinely don't know enough yet, and the discomfort is just accurate self-assessment. The question isn't whether you have doubts — it's whether those doubts are telling you something real.

What I've found more useful than the imposter syndrome frame is calibration. I always knew what I was doing. What changed over time wasn't confidence — it was knowing more precisely where on the scale I was operating. Some periods I was at a high level and I knew it. Other periods I was lower and I knew that too. That self-awareness is more useful than either manufactured confidence or unexamined doubt.

Document your accomplishments and positive feedback to counteract imposter syndrome when it strikes.

Keep a file of client testimonials, successful project outcomes, and professional recognition that you can review during moments of self-doubt.

Focus on the value you deliver to clients rather than comparing yourself to other marketers. Your unique perspective, systematic approach, and attention to detail create benefits that clients appreciate. You don't need to be the best marketer in the world to be valuable.

Share your knowledge and insights with others to build evidence of your expertise. Writing blog posts, speaking at events, or mentoring other marketers helps you recognize the knowledge you've developed and the value you provide.

Remember that clients hire you to solve their problems, not to be perfect. Your value comes from your ability to deliver results, not from having encyclopedic knowledge of every marketing technique ever developed.

Your Workspace Setup

Your workspace affects your ability to focus more than you probably realize. If you're neurodivergent, a poorly designed environment can turn simple tasks into exhausting battles. But most workspace advice assumes you have a neurotypical brain that can ignore distractions and adapt to any environment.

That's not how your brain works.

Your workspace needs to account for sensory sensitivities, attention differences, and executive function challenges. The good news is that once you get your environment right, everything else becomes easier.

Physical Space That Doesn't Drive You Nuts

The traditional office setup is designed for neurotypical brains. Open floor plans, fluorescent lighting, constant interruptions, and shared spaces assume you can filter distractions and maintain focus regardless of what's happening around you.

If you have ADHD, autism, or anxiety, this environment is torture.

My own workspace took years to get right. I converted my dining room into an office and spent a while figuring out what was actually wrong. The first problem was that my desk faced away from the door. That sounds like a small thing. It isn't. I keep my back to a wall everywhere I go — restaurants, waiting rooms, anywhere. Having my back to the door made the whole room feel off, and I couldn't work out why my focus was shot until I turned the desk around to face the room. Immediate difference.

The second problem was the fourth monitor. Three monitors wasn't enough, apparently, so I added a fourth mounted above the middle one. It looked impressive. It also turned the room into a furnace. I pulled it down and put the desk directly under the AC vent. Cold air, three screens, back to the wall, facing the room. Now it works.

The space is open but completely controlled. That word — controlled — matters more than I expected. When your brain is already doing extra work just to focus, you can't afford an environment that's fighting you.

You need a workspace that minimizes distractions, supports your sensory needs, and gives you control over your environment. This might mean fighting for accommodations at work or redesigning your home office completely.

Start with lighting. Fluorescent lights are the enemy of focus for many neurodivergent people. They flicker at frequencies that your brain notices even if you're not consciously aware of it. This creates subtle stress that builds throughout the day.

Replace harsh overhead lighting with softer alternatives. Use desk lamps with warm LED bulbs, floor lamps with diffused light, or even string lights if they help you feel calmer. Natural light is best when possible, but avoid glare on your computer screen.

Control your visual environment. Open floor plans and cluttered desks create visual noise that pulls your attention away from work. Your brain tries to process every visual stimulus, which depletes mental energy faster.

Face your desk toward a wall or window instead of a busy area. Use privacy screens or plants to block distracting views. Keep your desk surface clear except for what you're currently working on. Store everything else in drawers or organizers.

Address noise issues proactively. Background conversations, phone calls, keyboard clicking, and general office chatter all compete for your attention. Even if you think you're ignoring these sounds, your brain is still processing them.

Invest in good noise-canceling headphones or high-quality earplugs. Create white noise with a fan, air purifier, or ambient sound app. If you work in an office, request a quieter location or permission to work remotely when you need deep focus time.

Make your workspace comfortable for your body. Uncomfortable seating, poor monitor positioning, and inadequate desk space create physical stress that affects mental performance. You'll fidget more, take more breaks, and lose focus more easily.

Get a chair that supports your preferred sitting style. Some people focus better when they can rock or swivel slightly. Others need firm support and minimal movement. Adjust your monitor height so you're not craning your neck up or down.

Consider alternative seating options. Standing desks, balance balls, or even treadmill desks work well for some ADHD brains that need movement to focus. Test different options to find what helps you think better.

Create clear boundaries between work and non-work space. If you work from home, your brain needs to know when you're in work mode versus relaxation mode. This is important if you live in a small space.

Use a chair, lighting setup, or desk configuration that signals work time. Pack away work materials at the end of the day if you use a shared space. The physical act of transitioning helps your brain shift modes.

Store distracting items out of sight. That stack of books you've been meaning to read, the craft project you started last month, or the pile of mail on your desk all create mental noise. Put them somewhere you can't see them during work hours.

Digital Organization for Scattered Brains

Your digital workspace is just as important as your physical space. If your computer desktop looks like a tornado hit it, if you have 47 browser tabs open, and if you can't find files when you need them, you're creating unnecessary friction for your already-challenged executive function.

Neurodivergent brains often struggle with digital organization because we save everything "just in case," start projects without finishing them, and get distracted by interesting links before completing our original task.

Start with your computer desktop. A cluttered desktop creates the same visual noise as a messy physical desk. Your brain has to process all those icons every time you look at your screen.

Keep your desktop clear except for files you're actively working on today. Create a "Desktop Dump" folder where you quickly save things that land on your desktop, then sort through it weekly.

Use a simple folder structure that matches how you think, not how filing systems are "supposed" to work. If you think in terms of clients, organize by client names. If you think in terms of projects, organize by project types. Don't fight your natural mental categories.

My folder structure is: Clients > Client Name > Project Type > Year. This works for my brain because I remember who I was working with before I remember what type of project it was. Your structure might be different.

Manage browser tabs aggressively. Those 20+ open tabs aren't helping you multitask; they're creating decision fatigue every time you glance at your browser. Each tab represents an unfinished task that your brain is trying to track.

Use a "read later" app like Pocket or Instapaper for interesting articles you find. Bookmark useful resources instead of keeping tabs open. Close tabs as soon as you're done with them, even if you might need them later.

Set up your email for your attention style. If you check email compulsively, turn off notifications and check it at scheduled times only. If you forget to check email, set reminders or use an app that makes unread emails more visible.

Create email templates for common responses. This reduces the mental energy required for routine communication and helps you respond faster. I have templates for scheduling meetings, following up with prospects, and sending completed work to clients.

Use automation to reduce decisions. Set up automatic file backups, email filters that sort messages into folders, and calendar reminders for recurring tasks. Every automated process is one less decision your brain has to make.

Organize your files with clear, searchable names. "Client Proposal V3 Final FINAL" doesn't help future you find anything. Use consistent naming conventions like

"2024-03-15 Johnson Proposal Draft" so you can sort chronologically and find files quickly.

The Noise Problem (And Real Solutions)

Noise is probably the biggest workspace challenge for neurodivergent people. Your brain doesn't filter audio the same way neurotypical brains do. Background conversations, traffic sounds, air conditioning, and even the hum of electronics can pull your attention away from work.

The solution isn't just "use headphones." You need a comprehensive noise management strategy that works for your sensitivities and work requirements.

Identify your noise triggers first. Sudden sounds, repetitive sounds, human voices, and high-pitched noises affect people differently. Pay attention to what breaks your concentration and what helps you focus.

I can ignore traffic noise and air conditioning, but phone conversations in the next room destroy my ability to think. Instrumental music helps me focus, but anything with lyrics becomes distracting. Your triggers will be different.

Invest in quality noise-canceling headphones, not just any headphones. Active noise cancellation works best for steady, low-frequency sounds like air conditioning or traffic. It's less effective for sudden sounds or human voices, but it's still a huge improvement over regular headphones.

Try different types of background sound to find what works for your brain. Some people focus better with complete silence. Others need white noise, brown noise, nature sounds, or instrumental music. Experiment with different options.

Apps like Brain.fm, Noisli, or MyNoise offer different types of background audio designed for focus. Some ADHD brains focus better with slightly stimulating background noise, while others need calming sounds to reduce anxiety.

Create sound barriers in shared spaces. Use bookcases, plants, or portable screens to block sound transmission. Hang sound-absorbing materials like tapestries or acoustic panels if possible. Even small changes can make a difference.

Negotiate quiet hours if you work in an office. Ask if the team can minimize phone calls and conversations during times when you need to focus. Many workplaces are willing to accommodate this if you explain how it improves your productivity.

Use ear protection when necessary. High-quality earplugs or industrial ear protection can provide more noise reduction than headphones in very loud environments. Don't feel embarrassed about wearing them if they help you work better.

Consider timing your work around noise patterns. If your office is quieter early in the morning or late in the afternoon, schedule your most concentration-intensive tasks during those times. Work with your environment instead of fighting it.

Have backup plans for high-noise days. Identify alternative work locations like libraries, coffee shops with good Wi-Fi, or quiet areas in your building. Sometimes changing your location is easier than trying to control noise in your usual workspace.

Your workspace isn't just furniture and equipment. It's a tool that either supports your brain or fights against it. Spending time and money to optimize your environment isn't being picky or high-maintenance. It's being strategic about creating conditions where you can do your best work.

Most people underestimate how much their environment affects their performance because they've never experienced a truly optimized workspace. Once you get your setup right, you'll wonder how you ever managed to focus in chaotic environments.

Time Management That Doesn't Suck

Traditional time management assumes your brain works on a predictable schedule. Wake up at 6 AM, tackle your most important work first thing, maintain steady productivity throughout the day, and wrap up by 5 PM. Use time blocks, prioritize ruthlessly, and stick to your schedule no matter what.

If you're neurodivergent, this advice is about as useful as telling someone with depression to "just think positive thoughts."

Your brain doesn't operate on a corporate schedule. Your energy fluctuates unpredictably. Your hyperfocus kicks in at random times. Your executive function crashes when you need it most. Fighting these patterns is exhausting and counterproductive.

The solution isn't better discipline or more willpower. It's building time management systems that work with your brain instead of against it.

Forget Traditional Scheduling

The standard productivity advice tells you to plan your day in neat little time blocks. 9-10 AM for email, 10-12 PM for project work, 1-2 PM for meetings, 2-4 PM for administrative tasks. Each activity gets its assigned slot, and you move through your day like a well-oiled machine.

This works great if your brain can switch tasks on command and maintain consistent energy throughout the day. For neurodivergent brains, it's a recipe for frustration and failure.

For years I tried to work normal hours because everyone said that's how you do it. My most productive windows are 4 AM to 11 AM and 8 PM to midnight. Everyone I've told that to has some version of the same reaction: that's wrong, that's unsustainable, you need to normalize your schedule. I ignored all of it. This works for me. The rest of the advice doesn't. If you've found your windows, stop apologizing for them.

Your ADHD brain might want to spend four hours straight diving deep into research when you had scheduled 30 minutes for it. Your autistic brain might need longer transition time between different types of tasks. Your anxious brain might get stuck on one decision and throw off your entire schedule.

Instead of rigid time blocks, use flexible time containers. Block out general categories of work without start and end times. Create "admin morning," "creative afternoon," or "client work block" instead of "9:15-9:45 AM respond to emails."

This gives you structure without the stress of constant schedule violations. If responding to emails takes 20 minutes instead of 30, you're not behind. If it takes 45 minutes because of an urgent client issue, you're not scrambling to catch up.

Plan fewer things per day than you think you can accomplish. Neurodivergent brains are optimistic about time estimation and terrible at accounting for transition time, unexpected interruptions, and energy crashes. Cut your planned tasks in half.

I used to plan 8-10 tasks per day and feel like a failure when I completed 4. Now I plan 3-4 tasks per day and feel successful when I complete them all. Some days I get bonus tasks done. Most days I hit my target without stress.

Build buffer time around everything. Meetings, deadlines, travel time, even simple tasks like responding to emails. Buffer time accounts for the unexpected delays that always happen but somehow always surprise us.

If a client call is scheduled for 30 minutes, block 45 minutes on your calendar. If a project is due Friday, treat Thursday as your internal deadline. If it takes 20 minutes to drive somewhere, leave 30 minutes early.

Use natural break points instead of artificial time boundaries. Don't stop working on something just because your scheduled time block is over if you're in flow state. Don't force yourself to start a new task if you need transition time.

Plan your day around energy and attention patterns, not clock time. If you're sharpest in the morning, schedule your most challenging work then. If you hit your stride at 2 PM, protect that time for important projects.

Work with Your Weird Rhythms

Your brain has natural rhythms for energy, attention, and creativity. These rhythms don't match the standard 9-5 workday, and they might not even be consistent from day to day. Learning to recognize and work with these patterns improves your productivity and reduces stress.

Track your energy and attention patterns for at least a week. Note when you feel sharp and focused, when you're sluggish, when you're creative, and when you can only handle routine tasks. Look for patterns.

Most people discover they have 2-3 peak performance windows per day, separated by lower-energy periods. Your peaks might be 8-10 AM and 2-4 PM, or 10 AM-12 PM and 7-9 PM, or something different.

Protect your peak energy windows for your most important work. Don't waste these periods on email, administrative tasks, or routine maintenance. Use them for creative projects, complex problem-solving, or challenging client work.

Schedule low-energy tasks during your natural downtime. Email, filing, scheduling, and other administrative work can be done when your brain isn't firing on all cylinders. Save your peak periods for work that requires full mental engagement.

Accept that some days your rhythms will be off. Stress, lack of sleep, hormonal changes, weather, and dozens of other factors affect your energy patterns. Have backup plans for low-energy days.

On days when you can't focus on complex work, shift to maintenance tasks. Organize your files, update your website, respond to non-urgent emails, or plan future projects. You're still being productive, just in a different way.

Learn to recognize when you're forcing productivity versus when you're naturally productive. Forced productivity feels like pushing a boulder uphill. Natural productivity feels like riding a wave. Stop pushing boulders and start looking for waves.

Sometimes this means starting work at 6 AM because your brain is on fire. Sometimes it means taking a 3-hour break in the middle of the day and working until 8 PM. Sometimes it means working intensively for three days and barely working the fourth day.

If you work for yourself or have flexible arrangements, optimize your schedule around these patterns. If you work in a traditional office, look for ways to align your most important work with your peak periods, even if you can't control your overall schedule.

Use your low-energy periods for learning and inspiration. When you can't produce, consume. Read industry articles, watch educational videos, listen to podcasts, or browse competitor websites. This input often sparks ideas during your next productive period.

Emergency Deadline Protocols

Despite your best planning, you'll face emergency deadlines. A client moves up their launch date. A conference proposal is due tomorrow and you forgot about it. An urgent project lands on your desk with impossible timing.

Traditional advice tells you to just buckle down and push through. Work longer hours, skip breaks, drink more coffee, and force your way to the finish line. This approach might work once or twice, but it's not sustainable for neurodivergent brains.

You need emergency protocols that help you produce quality work under pressure without destroying your mental health.

First, assess whether the deadline is impossible or just uncomfortable. Sometimes what feels impossible is doable with the right approach. Other times, the deadline truly can't be met and you need to negotiate.

If the deadline is impossible, negotiate immediately. Explain what you can deliver by the requested date and offer alternatives. Most clients prefer honest communication over missed deadlines.

If the deadline is tight but doable, shift into crisis mode systematically. Don't just panic and work random long hours. Create a focused plan that maximizes your chances of success.

Clear everything else from your schedule. Cancel non-essential meetings, delegate what you can, and postpone everything that isn't critical. Your only job is meeting this deadline.

Break the project into the smallest possible pieces. Instead of "write proposal," break it down to "outline key points," "research competitor pricing," "draft executive summary," etc. Small tasks feel less overwhelming and create momentum.

Use time pressure as a focus tool. Set timer-based work sprints. Work for 25-45 minutes with complete focus, then take a 5-10 minute break. The time pressure can help your ADHD brain focus better than open-ended work sessions.

Eliminate perfectionism temporarily. The goal is good enough to meet the deadline, not perfect work that's delivered late. You can always improve it later if needed.

Take care of your basic needs even under pressure. Eat regularly, stay hydrated, and get some sleep. Your brain needs fuel to function, especially under stress. Skipping meals and pulling all-nighters usually makes you less productive, not more.

Have a recovery plan for after the deadline. Emergency sprints are exhausting. Plan lighter workloads, extra rest, and recovery time for the period after you deliver the work.

Build relationships with people who can help during crises. Other freelancers who can take overflow work, virtual assistants who can handle administrative tasks, or family members who can handle personal responsibilities while you focus on the deadline.

Learn from each emergency. Was this deadline avoidable with better planning? Did you underestimate how long the work would take? Are there warning signs you can watch for next time?

Project Management for Chaos Brains

Traditional project management assumes you think linearly. Start with a clear goal, break it into logical steps, estimate timeframes, assign resources, and execute the plan methodically. Monitor progress with Gantt charts and status reports. Adjust as needed and deliver on time.

If your brain is wired for chaos, this approach feels like trying to organize a tornado.

Your neurodivergent brain jumps between ideas, gets distracted by interesting tangents, forgets steps, and struggles with time estimation. You might hyperfocus on minor details while missing major deadlines. You see connections others miss but lose track of the basics.

The solution isn't forcing yourself into rigid project management frameworks. It's creating systems that use your chaotic thinking while keeping you moving toward your goals.

Breaking Down Overwhelming Projects

Large projects paralyze neurodivergent brains because we see everything at once. While neurotypical brains break complex tasks into manageable pieces, your brain gets overwhelmed by the sheer scope and doesn't know where to start.

The traditional advice is to create a work breakdown structure with hierarchical task lists. This works if you think in neat categories and logical sequences. If your brain sees projects as swirling clouds of interconnected possibilities, you need a different approach.

I tried every project management tool that got recommended to me — CRMs, task managers, all of it. The gurus were insistent. It made me crazy. There's nothing wrong with those tools for people whose brains work that way. Mine doesn't.

What actually works for me is a paper grid. I log steps as I complete them, not before. I'm not planning forward — I'm recording what happened. It sounds backwards. It works because I can see exactly where I am in a project at any moment without trusting a system I might have forgotten to update.

Start with brain dumping everything you can think of related to the project. Don't organize or prioritize yet. Just get every task, idea, concern, and requirement out of your head and onto paper or a digital document.

Write down obvious tasks like "create content" alongside random thoughts like "what if the client hates the color scheme" and technical concerns like "need to check browser compatibility." Include everything, no matter how small or tangential.

This brain dump serves two purposes. It clears mental clutter so you can think more clearly, and it ensures you don't lose important details that your scattered attention might otherwise forget.

Next, group related items without worrying about formal categories. Circle or highlight things that seem connected. You might have clusters around research, content creation, design, client communication, and technical setup. Let these categories emerge naturally instead of forcing predetermined buckets.

Now start identifying the minimum viable version of the project. What's the simplest thing you could deliver that would meet the requirements? This becomes your fallback plan if everything else goes wrong.

For a website redesign, the minimum might be updating the homepage with new content and fixing broken links. For a marketing campaign, it might be creating three social media posts and one email. Having this baseline reduces anxiety and gives you a starting point.

Break each cluster into tiny actions that take less than 30 minutes each. Instead of "write homepage copy," break it down to "research competitor messaging," "outline key benefits," "draft headline options," "write first paragraph," etc.

Neurodivergent brains often stall on vague tasks but can handle concrete actions. "Update website" feels overwhelming. "Change the phone number in the footer" feels doable.

Use the "next physical action" test for each task. If you wrote "plan social media strategy," ask yourself what the next physical action is. Maybe it's "open competitor Instagram accounts" or "create list of content topics." Keep breaking things down until each task describes something you could do right now.

Order tasks by energy and attention requirements, not just logical sequence. Group tasks that require similar mental states. Do all your research tasks when you're in research mode. Do all your writing when you're in creative mode. Do all your administrative tasks when you're in maintenance mode.

Visual Tracking That Makes Sense

Traditional project management relies heavily on text-based lists, spreadsheets, and timeline charts. These work well for linear thinkers but can be overwhelming for visual processors and pattern-recognition brains.

Your chaos brain needs to see the big picture and understand relationships between tasks. Static lists don't show you how pieces connect or help you spot patterns and dependencies.

Try a kanban board approach with columns for different stages: Ideas, Ready to Start, In Progress, Waiting for Feedback, and Done. This gives you a visual overview of where everything stands without complex scheduling.

You can use digital tools like Trello, Asana, or Notion, or create a physical board with sticky notes. Physical boards work well for people who need to touch and move things around. Digital boards work better if you need to access your projects from multiple locations.

Color-code tasks by type, priority, or energy level. Use red for urgent tasks, blue for creative work, green for administrative tasks, or whatever system makes sense to your brain. Colors help you identify what type of work you're looking at.

Some people color-code by how much mental energy a task requires. Green for easy tasks you can do when tired, yellow for moderate tasks that need some focus, red for complex tasks that require peak mental energy.

Use visual progress indicators that motivate you. Some people are motivated by completion percentages. Others prefer to see how many tasks they've moved to the "done" column. Some like to track streaks of productive days.

I use a simple progress bar for each major project area. Seeing the bar fill up as I complete tasks gives me a dopamine hit that motivates me to keep going. Find what visual feedback works for your brain.

Create visual connections between related tasks. Draw lines or arrows showing which tasks depend on others. Use different colors to show which tasks belong to the same project phase. This helps your pattern-recognition brain understand the project structure.

For complex projects, try mind mapping instead of linear task lists. Put the main project goal in the center and branch out with major categories, then branch again with tasks. This shows relationships and lets you see the whole project at once.

Track your energy and focus patterns alongside your task progress. Note which tasks you complete during high-energy periods versus low-energy periods. This helps you plan future projects around your natural rhythms.

Use time-boxing visually. Instead of detailed schedules, create visual blocks showing which types of work you'll do during different parts of the day or week. This gives structure without rigid timing.

How to Delegate When You're a Control Freak

I delegate like crazy when it makes sense. The operative phrase is "when it makes sense." Delegation isn't about offloading things you don't want to do — it's about being honest about what requires your brain and what doesn't.

But delegation without structure is just abdication. There are three things you have to get right or the whole thing falls apart.

First, give them a framework. Not a vague description of what you want — an actual framework. What does good look like? What are the steps? What do they do when something unexpected happens? If you can't explain the process clearly enough for someone else to follow it, you don't understand it well enough yourself yet.

Second, keep an eye on them. This isn't micromanagement — it's quality control. Check in at natural milestones. Review drafts before they go out. The goal is catching problems while they're still small, not hovering over every decision. There's a difference between monitoring and meddling. Learn it.

Third, make damn sure they know their responsibilities and their authority limits. This is where most delegation falls apart. The person doesn't know what they're allowed to decide on their own versus what needs to come back to you. That ambiguity costs you time, costs them confidence, and produces work that misses the mark. Be explicit. "You can approve anything under $500. Anything over that comes to me first." "You handle all client scheduling, but don't commit to timelines without checking." Whatever the limits are, state them clearly upfront.

The neurodivergent tendency is to either do everything yourself or hand things off completely and hope for the best. Both are wrong. Delegation is a system, and like every other system, it works when you build it properly and falls apart when you don't.

Communication Systems

Communication is exhausting for neurodivergent brains. You have to process social cues, remember conversational context, manage emotional reactions, and craft responses that won't be misunderstood. Meanwhile, your brain is already working overtime just to focus and organize your thoughts.

Traditional communication advice assumes you know how to read between the lines, respond appropriately to different personality types, and maintain professional relationships without explicit frameworks. If your brain doesn't come with these social operating instructions, every interaction becomes a complex puzzle to solve.

The solution isn't learning to communicate like a neurotypical person. It's building systems that reduce the cognitive load of communication while ensuring your message gets across clearly.

Email Templates That Save Your Sanity

Email is simultaneously the best and worst communication method for neurodivergent people. It's great because you can take time to craft responses and avoid real-time social processing. It's terrible because you can overthink every word, second-guess your tone, and spend hours writing messages that should take five minutes.

Email templates solve both problems. They give you tested frameworks that communicate effectively without requiring you to reinvent every message from scratch.

Full disclosure: I don't use templates. I write every email fresh depending on what I need it to do. Sometimes

I'll start with an AI draft and rewrite it completely. The point isn't that templates are wrong — it's that you need to know how you actually communicate and build around that, not around what you're supposed to do.

Start with templates for your most common email types. Client onboarding, project updates, meeting scheduling, proposal follow-ups, and invoice reminders probably account for 80% of your professional emails.

Your onboarding template might include: welcome message, next steps overview, timeline expectations, communication preferences, and what information you need from them. Having this structure ensures you don't forget important details when you're excited about a new project.

Create templates for different relationship stages. Your initial outreach email is different from your follow-up email, which is different from your "checking in after six months" email. Each stage requires different information and tone.

Build in personalization placeholders that force you to customize each message. Instead of sending generic templates, include spaces for project details, personal references from previous conversations, or industry examples.

My proposal follow-up template includes: "Thanks for taking the time to discuss [project detail from our conversation]" and "Based on your concern about [challenge they mentioned], I've included [relevant solution] in the proposal." This shows I was listening while saving me from writing every email from scratch.

Use templates to manage your tone consistency. When you're stressed, excited, frustrated, or distracted, your email tone can come across differently than you intend. Templates help you maintain professional communication regardless of your current mental state.

Create different templates for different communication styles. Some clients prefer detailed explanations. Others want brief updates. Some need lots of context. Others just want the key information. Having templates for each style lets you match their preferences without overthinking it.

Include boundary-setting language in your templates. "I respond to emails within 24 hours during business days" or "For urgent matters, please call [phone number]" sets clear expectations without requiring individual negotiations.

Build templates for difficult conversations. Declining projects, addressing scope creep, requesting payment, or delivering bad news all become easier when you have frameworks to follow. You can focus on the situation instead of figuring out how to phrase uncomfortable messages.

Your "scope creep" template might include: acknowledgment of their request, explanation of how it relates to the original scope, options for handling the additional work, and next steps. Having this structure prevents you from either agreeing to everything or sounding defensive.

Meeting Strategies That Don't Drain You

Meetings are designed for extroverted, neurotypical brains that can process multiple conversations simultaneously, think out loud, and maintain energy throughout long discussions. For neurodivergent people, meetings can be overwhelming, exhausting, and counterproductive.

But meetings are unavoidable in most marketing roles. You need strategies that help you participate effectively without depleting your energy reserves.

In every job I've had, meetings were a disaster — no agenda, people hijacking the conversation, sessions that wandered until someone called time. I came out of all that with one rule: 55 minutes maximum, agenda enforced, no detours. My meetings run tight. People who've sat in both kinds know the difference immediately.

Prepare for meetings more than others do. Review the agenda, research attendees, and think through potential discussion topics ahead of time. This preparation reduces the cognitive load during the meeting and helps you contribute meaningfully.

Write down key points you want to make before the meeting starts. Your brain might go blank when put on the spot, but having notes ensures you can contribute your ideas even if you don't think of them spontaneously.

Request agendas in advance and suggest structure when meetings lack clear objectives. "What decisions do we need to make in this meeting?" or "What outcomes are we hoping for?" help focus discussions and reduce time wasted on tangential conversations.

Position yourself strategically in the room or video call. Sit where you can see everyone without being in the center of attention. For video calls, position your camera so you're not constantly seeing yourself, which can be distracting.

Use the chat function in video meetings to participate when verbal contribution feels overwhelming. Many neurodivergent people process and express ideas better in writing than in real-time conversation.

Build in recovery time after meetings. Don't schedule back-to-back meetings or important work immediately after social interactions. Give yourself 15-30 minutes to decompress and process what happened.

Develop strategies for handling interruptions and fast-paced discussions. Some people use visual signals like raising their hand. Others write down their points and wait for natural breaks. Find what works for your communication style.

Take notes during meetings, even if someone else is the official note-taker. Writing helps many neurodivergent people process information and gives you something to focus on when the discussion becomes overwhelming.

Follow up after meetings with written summaries of your understanding. "Just to confirm, my next steps are X, Y, and Z, and we'll reconvene on [date] to discuss [topic]." This ensures you understood correctly and creates accountability.

Set boundaries around meeting frequency and duration. “I run all my meetings at 55 minutes” or “I prefer to batch my meetings on Tuesdays and Thursdays” helps others work with your needs.

Client Boundaries That Stick

Boundaries are important for neurodivergent marketers because we often struggle with people-pleasing, have difficulty reading social cues about appropriate requests, and may not recognize when clients are taking advantage of our willingness to help.

Your brain might not signal when someone is asking for too much, crossing professional lines, or making unreasonable demands. You need explicit frameworks for recognizing and addressing boundary violations.

Set clear communication boundaries from the beginning of every client relationship. Specify your preferred communication methods, response times, and availability. Include this information in your contracts and onboarding materials.

My communication boundaries include: email for non-urgent matters with 24-hour response time, phone calls scheduled in advance for complex discussions, and text messages only for true emergencies. I define "emergency" as something that costs money every hour it's not resolved.

Create boundaries around project scope and changes. "Additional requests outside the original scope will be handled through a separate project proposal" prevents scope creep from destroying your profitability and timeline.

Use templates for boundary conversations. When clients ask for work outside your scope, send a professional response that acknowledges their request, explains how it relates to your agreement, and offers options for moving forward.

Set financial boundaries that protect your business. Require deposits before starting work, establish payment terms that work for your cash flow, and have clear policies for late payments. Financial stress makes everything else harder for neurodivergent brains.

Build boundaries around your availability. Just because you can work evenings and weekends doesn't mean you should. Your brain needs downtime to recharge, and constant availability leads to burnout.

Create boundaries around client feedback and revisions. "Projects include two rounds of revisions based on the original brief" prevents endless revision cycles that exhaust your energy and erode your profits.

Use scripts for enforcing boundaries when clients push back. "I understand this feels urgent to you. Here's how we can handle it within our current agreement" or "I'd be happy to take on this additional work. Let me send you a proposal for the extra scope."

Document boundary violations and your responses. This helps you recognize patterns, improve your boundary-setting skills, and protect yourself if client relationships become problematic.

Address boundary violations immediately rather than letting them accumulate. Small violations that go unaddressed often escalate into larger problems that are harder to resolve.

Practice saying no in low-stakes situations so you're comfortable doing it when it matters. "No, I can't take on rush work this week" or "No, I don't work on weekends" become easier with practice.

Remember that good clients respect boundaries. Clients who consistently push against your professional limits aren't good fits for your business, regardless of how much they're willing to pay.

Communication systems for neurodivergent brains aren't about becoming a better communicator in the traditional sense. They're about creating structures that reduce the mental energy required for professional interactions while ensuring your message gets across clearly.

Using AI to Amplify Your Neurodivergent Brain

AI tools are perfect for neurodivergent marketers. They handle the routine cognitive tasks that drain your mental energy, help organize scattered thoughts into coherent strategies, and provide the executive function support that your brain sometimes lacks.

While neurotypical marketers might use AI to work faster, you can use it to work better. AI can be your external processing system, helping you manage the cognitive overhead that makes marketing exhausting for neurodivergent brains.

The key is understanding which tasks to delegate to AI and which to keep for yourself. Your human brain excels at pattern recognition, creative connections, and understanding nuanced client needs. AI excels at organization, consistency, and handling repetitive tasks that bog down your executive function.

AI as Your Executive Function Assistant

Executive function challenges make marketing feel overwhelming. You have brilliant ideas but struggle to organize them. You see the big picture but miss important details. You start projects enthusiastically but have trouble following through to completion.

AI can serve as your external executive function system, helping you break down complex projects, maintain consistency, and track progress without relying on your scattered attention.

Use AI to break down overwhelming projects into manageable tasks. Feed it your project description and ask for a detailed breakdown with action items. "I need to create a content marketing strategy for a B2B software company. Break this into tasks I can complete in 30-minute blocks."

AI will give you concrete steps like "research competitor content themes," "identify target audience pain points," "create content calendar template," and "draft three blog post outlines." This removes the mental burden of figuring out where to start.

Let AI help you create project timelines and dependencies. Your ADHD brain might see all tasks as equally urgent, but AI can help you identify which tasks need to happen first and how long each step takes.

Use AI to maintain consistency across your marketing materials. Feed it your brand guidelines, tone of voice examples, and key messaging, then ask it to review new content for consistency. This catches the details your scattered attention might miss.

AI can help you create templates and frameworks for recurring tasks. Instead of reinventing your approach every time, use AI to develop reusable structures for client onboarding, campaign planning, content creation, and project reporting.

Ask AI to help you anticipate problems and create contingency plans. "What could go wrong with this campaign timeline, and how should I prepare for potential issues?" This appeals to your anxious brain's need to plan for problems while being productive.

Use AI to track and analyze your own productivity patterns. Feed it your time tracking data and ask for insights about when you're most productive, which tasks take longer than expected, and how to optimize your schedule around your natural rhythms.

Content Creation and Idea Development

Your neurodivergent brain generates amazing ideas but struggles with execution. You see connections others miss but have trouble organizing those insights into coherent content. AI can bridge this gap by helping you develop and structure your creative thoughts.

Use AI as a brainstorming partner that never gets tired. When you're stuck on content ideas, feed it your target audience information, recent industry trends, and your unique perspective. Ask for 20 different angles on a topic, then choose the ones that spark your interest.

AI won't replace your creative insights, but it can help you explore ideas more systematically than your scattered brain might do alone. It can suggest angles you hadn't considered and help you see patterns in your thinking.

Let AI help you organize your stream-of-consciousness ideas into structured content. Dump all your thoughts about a topic into AI and ask it to organize them into a logical outline with clear sections and supporting points.

Use AI to adapt your content for different platforms and audiences. Your brain might generate one perfect explanation of a concept, but you need versions for LinkedIn, Twitter, email newsletters, and blog posts. AI can help you adjust tone, length, and format without starting from scratch.

AI can help you maintain content consistency when your brain jumps between different interests. Feed it your content themes and ask it to suggest how new ideas connect to your established topics. This keeps your content strategy coherent even when your attention wanders.

Use AI to flesh out incomplete ideas. When you have a spark of inspiration but can't develop it, AI can help you explore the concept from different angles and identify the most promising directions to pursue.

AI can also help you batch similar content creation tasks. Instead of writing one blog post at a time, use AI to help you create outlines for five related posts, then write them all in focused sessions.

Research and Data Analysis

Your pattern-recognition brain loves diving deep into research, but you can get lost in rabbit holes or overwhelmed by the sheer volume of information. AI can help you research more efficiently and organize findings in ways your brain can use.

Use AI to summarize long research documents and extract key insights. Instead of reading 50-page industry reports, feed them to AI and ask for summaries focused on questions relevant to your project.

AI can help you identify patterns across multiple data sources that your scattered attention might miss. Feed it competitor analysis data, customer feedback, and industry reports, then ask it to identify trends and opportunities.

Use AI to help you stay focused during research sessions. Ask it to generate research questions before you start, then use those questions to guide your investigation instead of following every interesting tangent.

AI can help you organize research findings into useful insights. Instead of ending up with a pile of interesting but disconnected information, use AI to help you synthesize your research into clear recommendations and next steps.

Let AI help you validate your intuitive insights with data. Your pattern-recognition brain often spots trends before they show up in formal research. Use AI to help you find supporting evidence for your hunches.

Use AI to help you communicate complex research findings to clients who don't share your deep-dive research style. AI can help you distill detailed analysis into executive summaries that highlight the most important points.

Administrative and Routine Tasks

Administrative tasks are the enemy of neurodivergent productivity. They're boring enough to trigger your avoidance mechanisms but important enough that you can't ignore them. AI can handle many of these tasks or make them less cognitively demanding.

Use AI to draft routine emails, proposals, and contracts. Feed it the key information and let it create professional drafts that you can review and personalize. This eliminates the blank page problem that often stalls your progress.

AI can help you manage your calendar and scheduling. Instead of the back-and-forth email dance of finding meeting times, use AI-powered scheduling tools that handle the logistics automatically.

Let AI help you track project progress and generate status reports. Feed it your project updates and let it create professional summaries for clients. This removes the mental burden of translating your scattered notes into coherent communication.

Use AI to automate social media posting and email marketing. Create content in batches when you're in creative mode, then let AI handle the consistent posting schedule that your ADHD brain struggles to maintain.

AI can help you organize your files and digital workspace. Use AI-powered tools to categorize documents, tag files with searchable keywords, and maintain the organizational systems that your executive function struggles to sustain.

Use AI to handle data entry and basic analysis tasks. Instead of manually updating spreadsheets or calculating metrics, use AI tools that can process information and generate reports automatically.

The goal isn't to replace your human creativity and insight with AI. It's to use AI as a cognitive support system that handles the routine mental overhead, leaving your brain free to focus on the creative, strategic, and relationship-building work where you excel.

AI tools work well for neurodivergent brains because they provide consistent support without judgment, never get tired of repetitive questions, and can adapt to your working style without requiring complex social negotiations.

Start small with one or two AI applications that address your biggest pain points, then gradually expand your AI toolkit as you become more comfortable with these tools.

Content Creation for Hyperfocusers

Content creation advice assumes you can maintain steady, consistent output. Write a little bit every day, post regularly on social media, and stick to your editorial calendar no matter what. This approach treats content creation like a factory assembly line where consistent input creates predictable output.

If you have ADHD or autistic hyperfocus tendencies, this advice is useless. Your brain doesn't work in steady, predictable rhythms. You have periods of intense creative energy followed by periods where forcing content feels impossible. You can spend eight hours writing the perfect blog post, then struggle to write a single social media caption for the next three days.

The solution isn't forcing yourself into artificial consistency. It's learning to work with your natural hyperfocus cycles to create better content more efficiently than neurotypical content creators ever could.

Batch Everything (The Right Way)

Batching content creation works well for hyperfocus brains, but not the way most productivity experts teach it. They suggest batching similar tasks together for efficiency. For hyperfocusers, batching is about capturing and channeling intense creative energy when it strikes.

Traditional batching advice tells you to write all your blog posts on Monday, create social media content on Tuesday, and record videos on Wednesday. This assumes you can schedule creative energy like a meeting. Your brain doesn't work that way.

Real batching for hyperfocusers means creating massive amounts of content when your brain is locked into creative mode, then having systems to publish and distribute that content during non-creative periods.

The most extreme example I have: when hyperfocus hits hard, I've worked sixteen hours straight and produced more than most people think is possible. I've written a complete novel in one of those sessions — not AI-assisted, just me. That's not a normal content workflow. It's mine. Fighting it was always the wrong call.

When hyperfocus kicks in for writing, don't just write one blog post. Write five. Create outlines for ten more. Draft email newsletters, social media captions, and video scripts. Capture everything your brain wants to create while the creative faucet is turned on.

The key is having systems ready before hyperfocus strikes. Create templates for different content types, set up folders for organizing drafts, and have publishing schedules prepared. When creative energy hits, you can focus on creation instead of figuring out logistics.

I keep content templates for blog posts, email newsletters, social media posts, and video scripts. When I'm hyperfocused on writing, I can fill these templates with ideas instead of starting from scratch every time. This lets me create more content in a single session.

Build content creation workflows that support long creative sessions. Set up your workspace with everything you need: research materials, style guides, image libraries, and reference documents. Remove friction so you can stay in flow state as long as possible.

Create different batching strategies for different types of hyperfocus. Visual hyperfocus might produce dozens of social media graphics in one session. Research hyperfocus might generate material for months of educational content. Writing hyperfocus might create entire content series.

Don't try to force batching when your brain isn't in creative mode. Use low-energy periods for content organization, publishing, and distribution instead of creation. Your hyperfocus sessions produce the raw material; your maintenance periods handle the logistics.

Document your hyperfocus patterns so you can prepare for them. If you tend to get writing-focused on Sunday mornings or visual-creative on Wednesday afternoons, protect those times and have your systems ready.

Turn Your Obsessions Into Content Gold

Neurodivergent brains develop intense interests in topics that might seem random to others. You might become obsessed with conversion rate optimization, fascinated by email deliverability, or deeply interested in color psychology. These obsessions are content goldmines that most marketers ignore.

Your deep dives into narrow topics give you expertise that surface-level content creators can't match. While others are recycling the same generic advice, you're exploring nuances and connections that create valuable content.

Map your current obsessions and interests to potential content themes. What topics do you research for fun? What rabbit holes do you fall into during downtime? What subjects can you talk about for hours without getting bored?

My content themes emerged from my obsessions: email marketing automation workflows, landing page psychology, and conversion optimization testing. These weren't strategic business decisions; they were topics I couldn't stop thinking about anyway.

Use your research obsessions as content inspiration. When you spend three hours researching a technical detail for a client project, turn that research into educational content. You've already done the hard work; creating content from it is just repackaging.

Create content series around your deep interests. Instead of surface-level posts about general marketing topics, create detailed explorations of subjects you find fascinating. Your enthusiasm for the topic will come through and attract audiences who share your interests.

Don't worry about whether your obsessions seem "marketable" at first. Niche expertise often leads to more engaged audiences than broad, generic content. People who care deeply about your obsession will become devoted followers.

Document your learning process as content. When you're diving deep into a new topic, create content about what you're discovering. "What I learned from analyzing 100 email subject lines" or "5 surprising insights from A/B testing button colors" turns your research into shareable content.

Use your pattern-recognition abilities to spot connections others miss. Your brain sees relationships between seemingly unrelated topics. These unique perspectives create content that stands out from the crowd.

Connect your obsessions to broader marketing principles. Your deep dive into email deliverability can become content about attention to detail in marketing. Your fascination with conversion psychology can become content about understanding customer behavior.

Consistency Without Burnout

The biggest challenge for hyperfocus content creators is maintaining consistent publishing without burning out. Your creative energy comes in bursts, but your audience expects regular content. You need systems that smooth out your irregular creative cycles.

Build content buffers during hyperfocus periods. When you're in creative mode, create enough content to sustain publishing during low-energy periods. Aim for 4-6 weeks of buffer content so you're never scrambling to create something when your creative energy is depleted.

Use scheduling tools to maintain consistent posting even when you're not creating. Tools like Buffer, Hootsuite, or Later let you queue up content during productive periods and maintain regular posting schedules automatically.

Create content frameworks that you can fill in during different energy states. High-energy periods are for original creation. Medium-energy periods are for adapting existing content for different platforms. Low-energy periods are for simple tasks like scheduling and organizing.

Develop "emergency content" for periods when your creative energy crashes. Curated content, behind-the-scenes posts, or simple question posts can maintain your publishing schedule without requiring intense creative effort.

My emergency content includes: industry article roundups, "what I'm reading" posts, simple polls asking audience questions, and repurposed snippets from previous content. These require minimal creative energy but keep my publishing schedule consistent.

Accept that some periods will be less creative than others. Instead of forcing creation during low-energy times, focus on content distribution, audience engagement, and system optimization. These activities still move your content strategy forward without depleting your creative reserves.

Use your hyperfocus periods strategically. Don't waste intense creative energy on routine content that could be created during lower-energy periods. Save hyperfocus sessions for your most important, complex, or innovative content pieces.

Track your creative energy patterns alongside your content output. Understanding when you're most creative helps you plan content creation sessions and set realistic publishing schedules that work with your natural rhythms.

Build flexibility into your content calendar. Instead of rigid posting schedules, create ranges: "post 2-3 times per week" instead of "post every Monday, Wednesday, Friday." This reduces pressure while maintaining general consistency.

Create content recycling systems that extend the life of your hyperfocus creations. One deep-dive blog post can become a newsletter series, multiple social media posts, a video script, and a podcast episode outline. This maximizes the value of your intense creative sessions.

Remember that quality matters more than quantity for building engaged audiences. Your hyperfocus-created content will be more thorough, more insightful, and more valuable than content created under artificial time pressure. Let this quality compensate for occasional irregular posting.

Data and Analytics for Pattern Brains

Most marketers treat data analysis like a chore. They pull reports, glance at the numbers, and move on to more "creative" work. They see analytics as a necessary evil rather than a source of insight and competitive advantage.

If you're neurodivergent, data analysis might be one of your secret weapons. Your pattern-recognition brain excels at spotting trends, connections, and anomalies that others miss. Your obsessive attention to detail catches insights hiding in the numbers. Your systematic thinking helps you build analytical frameworks that produce reliable results.

The challenge isn't analyzing data—it's knowing which data to analyze and how to communicate your insights to people who don't share your love of spreadsheets and statistical significance.

Which Metrics Matter

Data overwhelm is real for pattern-recognition brains. You can see interesting correlations everywhere, get distracted by statistical outliers, and lose hours investigating fascinating but irrelevant data points. Every metric seems important when you can see how it connects to everything else.

The solution isn't ignoring data. It's focusing your analytical powers on metrics that drive business decisions rather than satisfying intellectual curiosity.

I learned this the hard way. Early on I was tracking hits and views religiously, celebrating when a post hit 100,000 views. It felt like proof something was working. It wasn't. Zero conversions. I spent a long time chasing a number that had no relationship to income before I understood the metric was irrelevant. Now I only track what connects to money in or money out. Everything else is noise until proven otherwise.

Start with outcome metrics that impact business goals. Revenue, profit margins, customer acquisition cost, lifetime value, and conversion rates are the numbers that matter to clients and stakeholders. Everything else is supporting data.

Your pattern brain will want to dive into every possible correlation, but resist the urge until you understand these fundamental metrics. You can explore interesting patterns after you've covered the basics that people expect in your reports.

Choose 3-5 key performance indicators for each campaign or project. More than that creates decision paralysis for stakeholders who don't process data the same way you do. Fewer than that might miss important insights.

For a content marketing campaign, your core metrics might be: traffic growth, email signups, content engagement rate, lead quality score, and cost per lead. These tell a complete story without overwhelming your audience with data.

Focus on metrics you can influence through your marketing activities. Website visitor counts are interesting, but visitors from traffic sources helps you optimize your efforts. Monitoring social media followers is nice, but tracking followers who convert to customers actually tells you something.

Distinguish between vanity metrics and performance metrics. Vanity metrics make you feel good but don't drive business decisions. Performance metrics might be less exciting but help you improve results.

Page views, social media likes, and email open rates are often vanity metrics. They can indicate progress but don't correlate with business outcomes. Conversion rates, customer acquisition costs, and revenue per visitor are performance metrics that guide optimization decisions.

Build custom metrics that reflect your unique value proposition. If you're selling efficiency improvements, track time-saved metrics. If you're focused on quality, develop quality score systems. Create measurements that align with what you're promising to deliver.

Track leading indicators alongside lagging indicators. Lagging indicators tell you what happened. Leading indicators help you predict what will happen. Both are important for different types of decisions.

Email signups are a leading indicator for future sales. Revenue is a lagging indicator of past marketing effectiveness. Tracking both helps you optimize current campaigns while measuring historical performance.

Spreadsheet Systems That Work

Your neurodivergent brain probably loves spreadsheets for their logical structure and analytical possibilities. But without proper organization systems, your spreadsheets can become overwhelming digital hoards that hide insights instead of revealing them.

Create template spreadsheets for recurring analysis tasks. Campaign performance tracking, client reporting, competitive analysis, and project ROI calculations probably follow similar patterns each time. Templates ensure consistency and reduce setup time for new projects.

My campaign tracking template includes: traffic source, visitor count, conversion rate, cost per click, cost per conversion, revenue generated, and ROI calculation. I can copy this template for every campaign and compare performance across time periods.

Use consistent naming conventions for files, tabs, and columns. Your future self will thank you when you can locate data instead of hunting through cryptically named files. Include dates in filenames and use descriptive tab names.

Color-code your spreadsheets systematically. Green for positive performance, red for concerning trends, yellow for data that needs attention. This visual system helps you identify patterns without reading every number.

Build automated calculations wherever possible. Let Excel or Google Sheets handle the math so you can focus on analysis and interpretation. Use formulas for conversion rates, percentage changes, and other routine calculations.

Create data validation rules to prevent errors. Dropdown menus for categorical data, date formatting for time-based entries, and number formatting for metrics prevent the data entry mistakes that can invalidate your analysis.

Separate raw data from analysis and presentation. Keep source data on one tab, calculations on another, and charts or summaries on a third. This protects your raw data while making it easy to update analysis when new data arrives.

Document your methodology within the spreadsheet. Include notes explaining how you calculated metrics, what date ranges you used, and any assumptions you made.

This helps others understand your analysis and helps you remember your approach months later.

Use pivot tables to explore patterns without destroying your original data structure. Pivot tables let you slice and dice data multiple ways while keeping your source data intact. They're perfect for the exploratory analysis that pattern brains love.

Presenting Data to Neurotypical Teams

Your analytical brain can spot dozens of interesting insights in a single dataset. You see correlations, trends, and implications that excite you intellectually. But when you present these findings to neurotypical stakeholders, you often get blank stares or requests to "just give me the bottom line."

The problem isn't that your insights are wrong. It's that you're presenting analysis the way you like to consume it rather than the way your audience needs to receive it.

Start with the conclusion, not the methodology. Lead with the key insight or recommendation, then provide supporting data for people who want details. Most stakeholders need to know what action to take before they care about how you reached that conclusion.

Instead of: "I analyzed 47 different metrics across 12 traffic sources over 6 months and found several interesting correlations..."

Try: "We should shift 30% of our advertising budget from Facebook to Google Ads because it will reduce our customer acquisition cost by $23 per customer."

Use the "So what?" test for every data point you present. If you can't explain why a metric matters for business decisions, don't include it in stakeholder presentations. Save interesting but non-useful insights for separate discussions with fellow data enthusiasts.

Create visual hierarchies that guide attention to the most important information. Use larger fonts, bold text, or contrasting colors for key metrics. Present supporting data in smaller text or secondary charts.

Limit yourself to 3-5 key insights per presentation. Your brain can process complex multi-dimensional analysis, but most people need time to absorb each insight before moving to the next one. Dense presentations overwhelm decision-makers and reduce the impact of your recommendations.

Tell stories with your data instead of just presenting numbers. Connect metrics to business outcomes, customer experiences, or competitive advantages. Help stakeholders understand not just what the numbers say, but why those numbers matter.

"Email open rates increased 15%" is a statistic. "Our new subject line strategy helped 300 more customers discover our weekly tips, leading to 45 additional sales" is a story that shows business impact.

Prepare for questions by anticipating skepticism and requests for additional detail. Stakeholders might challenge your methodology, ask for different time periods, or want to see the data cut different ways. Have backup slides or data ready for these follow-up questions.

Use executive summaries for complex analysis. Create one-page overviews that highlight key findings, recommendations, and supporting evidence. Link to detailed analysis for people who want to dive deeper, but don't force everyone through your complete methodology.

Practice translating technical insights into business language. Instead of "statistically significant correlation," say "strong relationship." Instead of "confidence interval," say "we're confident this result will hold." Match your language to your audience's expertise level.

Build credibility by acknowledging limitations and uncertainties in your analysis. Your analytical brain probably sees potential flaws or alternative explanations that others miss. Addressing these proactively shows intellectual honesty and builds trust in your recommendations.

Your neurodivergent brain gives you analytical superpowers that most marketers lack. The key is channeling those powers toward useful insights that help clients and stakeholders make better decisions.

Social Media Without Overwhelm

Social media is useful and dangerous in equal measure. Useful because it puts you in front of people who don't know you exist yet. Dangerous because you're building on someone else's land. Any platform can change its algorithm, kill your reach, or disappear entirely on a corporate whim. It has happened to people who built their entire business there. Don't be those people.

The rule is simple: your website first, always. That's your land. You own it. Social media is how you drive traffic to it — not where you live. Every post, every engagement, every follower you build on someone else's platform should be pointing back to something you control.

From there, be selective. I use LinkedIn and Facebook. That's it. YouTube was a massive time sink with minimal return for the kind of business I run. X is a cesspool I don't need in my life. You don't have to be everywhere. You have to be where your clients actually are, and you have to show up with something worth seeing.

Here's what most social media advice gets wrong: people don't go to social media for information. They go for emotion. They want to feel something — inspired, relieved, seen, entertained. If you're posting tips and tactics and industry insights, you're giving people what you think they should want. Post your wins. Post your failures. Post testimonials. Post the thing that happened yesterday that made you think. That's what actually moves people.

Automation That Doesn't Sound Robotic

Automation handles the logistics so you can focus on the content that matters. Batch create during your high-energy periods and schedule from there. The trap is over-automating — scheduling generic posts that nobody asked for and wondering why nothing is happening. Automation keeps you consistent. It doesn't replace having something real to say.

My content rotates between case studies, wins, failures, client results, and behind-the-scenes glimpses of how I work. No tips listicles. No "5 ways to" posts. That content is everywhere and nobody remembers it. The posts people share are the ones where they felt something.

Schedule your posting but handle your engagement personally. When someone comments or messages you, that's a human being. Respond like one. The automation is for getting content out the door consistently — not for replacing the actual relationship.

Community Building for Introverts

You don't need a massive following. You need the right people paying attention. A hundred people who genuinely care about what you do are worth more than ten thousand followers who scroll past you without stopping.

Build on LinkedIn and Facebook if that's where your clients are. Don't chase platforms because a guru told you they're the future. Chase the platform where you can actually reach the people who hire people like you.

Post things that are true. A client result with real numbers. A mistake you made and what you learned. A testimonial that shows what it's actually like to work with you. These posts don't go viral often, but they convert. Someone reads that you turned around a failing campaign and thinks "that's exactly what I need." That's the point.

For neurodivergent marketers who hate performing extroversion online, this approach is a relief. You're not trying to be charming or entertaining or witty on demand. You're just being honest about your work. That's sustainable. The performance exhausts you. The honesty doesn't.

When to Ignore Engagement

Likes and follower counts are not business metrics. Revenue is a business metric. I spent enough time celebrating posts with massive reach and zero conversions to know the difference. The number that matters is how many people contacted you, hired you, or bought from you. Everything else is vanity unless you can draw a direct line from that engagement to actual income.

Check your metrics on a schedule, not compulsively. Once a week is enough. What you're looking for is direction — which types of posts generate real conversations, which ones generate inquiries, which ones do nothing. Let that guide what you keep doing, not the dopamine hit of a post that blew up and produced nothing.

The other thing to ignore: engagement bait. Polls, fill-in-the-blank posts, "comment below" tactics. They generate noise that looks like momentum and means nothing. Your time is finite. Spend it on content that could actually bring someone to your website and into your world.

One more thing about platform risk. Build an email list in parallel with everything else. When LinkedIn changes its algorithm or Facebook decides your organic reach is now zero, your email list is still yours. That list is the only social media asset you actually own. Treat it accordingly.

Campaign Strategy for Systems Thinkers

Most campaign strategy advice is built for people who love planning. Detailed timelines, customer journey maps, multi-stage funnels with decision trees. If you have ADHD, this is a trap. You can spend weeks building the perfect campaign architecture and never actually launch anything. The plan becomes the procrastination.

The antidote is simple: start with your audience and build outward from there. Not your message, not your channel, not your creative concept — your audience. Who are they, what do they actually need, and where are they already paying attention? Answer those three questions and the rest of the campaign follows naturally. Skip them and you're just guessing with better graphics.

Building Campaigns That Make Sense

Pick your audience before you pick anything else. Not a demographic — a specific person with a specific problem you know how to solve. The more precisely you can describe who you're talking to, the less work everything else in the campaign has to do.

Then build the campaign around them. What do they need to see first to know you exist? What do they need to believe before they'll contact you? What objection is sitting between them and a decision? Answer those questions and you have a campaign. Everything else — the channels, the content, the timing — is just execution against those answers.

Keep the structure simple. Awareness first, then consideration, then conversion. That's it. Neurodivergent brains can see every possible path through a campaign simultaneously, which makes the temptation to map all of them almost irresistible. Resist it. Build the main path. Get it live. Add complexity later if the data says to.

Set one primary metric before you launch. Not five metrics, not a dashboard — one. The number that tells you whether this campaign is working or not. Everything else is context. That one number is the verdict.

Contingency Planning (Because Things Break)

When a campaign isn't working, kill it. This is harder than it sounds. You've invested time and money and mental energy, and the sunk cost feels real. It isn't. What's real is the ongoing cost of running something that isn't producing results.

The question isn't "should I give it more time?" The question is "what would have to be true for this to work?" If the answer requires the audience to behave differently than they're behaving, or the market to change, or you to get lucky — kill it. If the answer is a specific tweak you can test in a week, test it. One test. If that doesn't move the number, kill it.

Build kill criteria before you launch. Decide in advance: if we hit this date and the metric is below this number, we stop. Making that decision before you're emotionally invested in the campaign means you'll actually follow through on it. Making it mid-campaign, when you're hoping it turns around, means you won't.

Budget a contingency reserve — 15 to 20 percent — for tests and adjustments. Campaigns rarely run exactly as planned. Having room to maneuver means a bad start doesn't automatically become a failed campaign.

Long-term Thinking Without Getting Lost

The ADHD mind is very good at seeing long-term possibilities and very bad at staying focused on them long enough to get there. The fix is not more strategic planning — it's shorter feedback loops.

Instead of a six-month campaign plan, run six-week sprints with clear objectives. At the end of each sprint, evaluate what you learned and decide what the next one looks like. This keeps you moving toward a long-term goal without requiring you to maintain enthusiasm for a plan you made two months ago under completely different circumstances.

Document what works. Not in a system you'll never look at — in something simple you'll actually use. What audience responded? What message landed? What channel produced actual leads? That knowledge compounds. The marketer who knows what worked for them last year is at a permanent advantage over the one starting from scratch every time.

The systematic mind excels at campaign strategy when it stays in motion. Plan enough to launch. Launch. Learn. Adjust. The marketers who overthink and never ship lose to the ones who ship and iterate every single time.

Networking Without Wanting to Die

Traditional networking advice assumes you're social, enjoy meeting strangers, and can work a room full of people without breaking into a cold sweat. You're supposed to attend every industry event, collect business cards like Pokemon, and maintain superficial relationships with hundreds of contacts.

If you're neurodivergent, this approach to networking feels like social torture. Large groups drain your energy. Small talk feels forced and meaningless. Networking events are loud, overwhelming, and full of unclear social expectations. You'd rather focus on your work than schmooze with strangers who might never become clients.

But networking is unavoidable in marketing. Relationships drive referrals, partnerships, and opportunities. You need strategies that let you build professional connections without destroying your mental health or pretending to be someone you're not.

Find Your Marketing People

The networking advice to "attend everything and meet everyone" is terrible for neurodivergent brains. You don't have unlimited social energy, and not all networking opportunities are worth your time. You need to be strategic about where you invest your relationship-building efforts.

Start by identifying your ideal networking targets. Who are the people that could help your business grow? Who shares your professional interests? Who works with your target clients but doesn't compete with you?

For a content marketing specialist, valuable networking contacts might include web designers, marketing automation consultants, sales trainers, and business coaches. These people work with similar clients but offer complementary services.

My networking script came from Royce Blake, who taught me a framework I've used ever since: introduce yourself, add something personal, then lead with what's in it for them. Not what you do, not your credentials — the specific value the other person might get from knowing you. Most people walk into networking conversations thinking about themselves. That reframe changes everything.

I stick to small groups and structured formats. BNI-style meetings work better for me than open mixers — though BNI itself is a different story. The point is the format: structured, time-limited, everyone gets a turn. I control my part of it and go home.

Look for industry groups rather than generic business networking organizations. General networking groups attract every type of business owner, making conversations scattered and less relevant to your needs. Industry groups focus discussions on topics you care about.

Join online communities before attending in-person events. Facebook groups, LinkedIn communities, Slack channels, and industry forums let you identify interesting people and start conversations before meeting face-to-face. This reduces the pressure of starting from scratch at live events.

Seek out smaller, more focused gatherings instead of large networking events. Mastermind groups, intimate workshops, and small meetups create better environments for meaningful conversations. You can get to know people instead of exchanging business cards with strangers.

Connect with other neurodivergent entrepreneurs and marketers. They understand your challenges, share similar working styles, and often make better collaborators than neurotypical contacts who don't understand your needs.

Follow the 80/20 rule for networking activities. Spend 80% of your networking energy maintaining and deepening existing relationships, and only 20% meeting new people. Strong relationships with a few key contacts are more valuable than weak connections with hundreds of acquaintances.

Use your interests and expertise as networking filters. If you're obsessed with email marketing automation, find communities where people discuss marketing technology. If you love data analysis, connect with other analytical marketers. Your genuine enthusiasm for these topics makes networking feel more natural.

Conference Survival Tactics

Conferences are necessary evils for most marketing careers. They're where industry trends emerge, where partnerships form, and where you learn about new opportunities. But they're also overwhelming sensory experiences designed for extroverted networking styles.

You can't avoid conferences entirely, but you can approach them strategically to maximize value while minimizing stress.

Choose conferences carefully based on clear objectives. Don't attend events just because they're well-known or because everyone else is going. Pick conferences that align with your learning goals, offer valuable networking opportunities, or provide business development benefits.

Plan your conference schedule in advance rather than trying to attend everything. Review the agenda, identify the most valuable sessions, and leave buffer time between activities. Trying to maximize every minute leads to burnout and reduces the quality of your experience.

Book accommodations that give you a retreat space. A quiet hotel room where you can recharge between activities is essential. Consider staying an extra night so you can recover before returning to normal work responsibilities.

Arrive early to get oriented before crowds arrive. Scope out quiet spaces where you can retreat when you need breaks. Identify less crowded areas for conversations. Plan your routes between session rooms to avoid getting lost in chaos.

Set realistic networking goals instead of trying to meet everyone. Aim for 3-5 meaningful conversations rather than collecting dozens of business cards. Quality connections matter more than quantity for building lasting professional relationships.

Use meal times strategically for networking. Instead of attending large networking lunches, schedule one-on-one meals with people you want to know better. This turns necessary eating time into valuable relationship building without the chaos of group dining.

Prepare your introduction and conversation topics ahead of time. Having a mental script reduces the cognitive load of social interaction and ensures you communicate your value clearly even when you're drained.

Take regular breaks between sessions. Step outside for fresh air, find a quiet corner to process information, or retreat to your hotel room. Don't push through until you're depleted.

Use technology to enhance your networking efficiency. Connect with people on LinkedIn before or after meeting them. Use conference apps to schedule meetings in advance. Take photos of business cards so you can throw away the physical cards.

Online Networking That Works

Online networking often works better for neurodivergent professionals because it removes many of the challenges of face-to-face interaction. You can take time to craft thoughtful responses, avoid overwhelming social environments, and build relationships at your own pace.

Focus on platforms where thoughtful content performs well. LinkedIn rewards professional insights and industry commentary. Twitter allows for quick exchanges around trending topics. Industry forums encourage detailed discussions about technical subjects.

Share valuable content consistently rather than only posting when you need something. Educational insights, industry observations, behind-the-scenes content, and helpful resources attract people to your network organically.

Engage with other people's content instead of just broadcasting your own messages. Comment thoughtfully on posts that interest you, share content that adds value to your network, and participate in discussions where you have genuine insights to contribute.

Use direct messages to deepen relationships that start in public forums. Many neurodivergent people are more comfortable with one-on-one conversations than group discussions. Use public interactions as springboards for private conversations.

Create valuable resources that attract your ideal networking contacts. Comprehensive guides, useful templates, or industry research draw people to you instead of requiring you to reach out constantly. Let your expertise do the networking work.

Host virtual events around topics you're passionate about. Webinars, online workshops, or digital meetups let you share knowledge while building relationships in structured formats that feel more manageable than casual networking.

Join or create mastermind groups with other professionals at similar career stages. These ongoing relationships provide accountability, advice, and collaboration opportunities without the pressure of constant networking activities.

Use scheduling tools to manage networking conversations efficiently. Instead of endless email exchanges trying to find meeting times, use tools like Calendly to let people book time with you.

Follow up systematically after online interactions. Send LinkedIn connection requests with personal notes referencing your conversation. Add new contacts to your CRM system. Set reminders to check in periodically with valuable connections.

Build email lists from your networking activities. Offer valuable resources in exchange for email addresses, then maintain relationships through regular newsletters or updates. This creates ongoing contact without requiring constant social media engagement.

Remember that online networking is about building real relationships, not just accumulating followers. Focus on providing value, being helpful, and maintaining consistent contact with people who matter to your business.

Client Management

Client management is challenging for neurodivergent marketers. You might struggle with reading social cues about client satisfaction, have difficulty setting boundaries without feeling guilty, or get overwhelmed by conflicting feedback that doesn't make logical sense.

Your people-pleasing tendencies can lead to scope creep that destroys profitability. Your perfectionist streak might cause you to over-deliver to the point of burnout. Your rejection sensitivity can make critical feedback feel like personal attacks rather than business discussions.

But client management isn't about becoming more assertive or developing thicker skin. It's about creating systems and frameworks that protect your business while building strong professional relationships.

Setting Boundaries That Stick

Boundaries aren't suggestions or preferences. They're the operational requirements that let you deliver quality work sustainably. Without clear boundaries, client relationships become chaotic, unprofitable, and stressful.

The challenge for neurodivergent marketers is that boundary violations often happen gradually through small requests that seem reasonable individually but add up to major scope changes.

I once fired a client worth $190,000 before the project really got going. The signals were there early — controlling behavior, the kind where every small decision becomes a negotiation. I've seen how that plays out. The money sounds significant until you calculate what it costs in time, stress, and the work you can't take on because you're managing someone who doesn't want to be managed. I made the call early.

Document your boundaries in contracts and onboarding materials. Don't assume clients understand your working style or availability. Spell out communication methods, response times, project scope, revision limits, and change request procedures.

My boundaries include: email for non-urgent communication with 24-hour response time, scheduled phone calls for complex discussions, no weekend work except for pre-arranged rush projects, and all scope changes require written approval before implementation.

Communicate boundaries as business requirements, not personal preferences. "I work most effectively when communications come through email" sounds like you're being difficult. "Our project management system requires email documentation to ensure nothing gets missed" sounds like good business practice.

Set financial boundaries that protect your cash flow and profitability. Require deposits before starting work, establish clear payment terms, and have policies for late payments. Financial stress makes everything else harder for neurodivergent brains.

Build buffer time into all project timelines to account for scope creep, revision requests, and unexpected complications. Underpromise on timelines so you can overdeliver without destroying your schedule when projects expand beyond original expectations.

Create standardized responses for common boundary situations. When clients ask for rush work, request additional services, or want communication outside your preferred methods, have professional responses ready that redirect them toward your established processes.

Use contracts and project agreements to enforce boundaries without personal confrontation. "According to our agreement, additional requests like this are handled through a separate project proposal" removes emotion from boundary enforcement.

Address boundary violations immediately rather than letting them accumulate. Small violations that go unaddressed often escalate into larger problems that are harder to resolve. Quick correction prevents bigger conflicts later.

Track boundary violations and client responses to identify patterns. Some clients consistently push boundaries and may not be good long-term fits. Others respect boundaries once they understand them and become ideal clients.

Handling Difficult Feedback

Feedback feels personal when you're neurodivergent. Your brain might interpret criticism of your work as criticism of your intelligence, competence, or worth. Rejection sensitivity can turn routine revision requests into emotional crises that derail your productivity.

The solution isn't developing thicker skin. It's creating mental frameworks that help you process feedback objectively and respond professionally even when your emotions are triggered.

Separate feedback about work from feedback about you as a person. "This headline doesn't capture our brand voice" is information about the headline, not a judgment about your writing ability. "We need to try a different approach" means the strategy needs adjustment, not that you're a bad strategist.

Ask clarifying questions to understand what clients want changed. Vague feedback like "make it more engaging" or "it doesn't feel right" doesn't give you clear direction. Push for changes you can implement.

"More engaging" might mean shorter paragraphs, more concrete examples, stronger headlines, or different tone. "Doesn't feel right" might mean the messaging is off-brand, the timing feels rushed, or the call-to-action isn't clear enough.

Request examples when possible. If they want "more professional" design, ask them to share examples of designs they consider professional. If they want "more compelling" copy, ask for examples of compelling content in their industry.

Document all feedback and decisions to prevent confusion later. When clients change their minds or forget previous discussions, written records protect you from endless revision cycles and scope creep.

Respond to feedback with questions and options rather than immediate implementation. "I understand you want the headline to be more compelling. Would you prefer we focus on the financial benefits, the time savings, or the competitive advantage?" This ensures you're solving the right problem.

Set limits on revision rounds to prevent perfectionist clients from requesting endless changes. "Projects include two rounds of revisions based on the original brief" creates structure around the feedback process.

Take time to process emotional reactions before responding to difficult feedback. Your initial reaction might be defensive, hurt, or frustrated. Let those feelings settle before crafting your professional response.

Use feedback as learning opportunities rather than personal failures. Each piece of criticism teaches you something about client preferences, market expectations, or areas where you can improve your skills.

When to Fire Clients (And How)

Firing clients feels impossible when you struggle with people-pleasing or worry about your reputation. But keeping bad clients is worse for your business than losing their revenue. Problem clients drain energy, destroy profitability, and prevent you from serving good clients effectively.

Learn to recognize the warning signs of clients who aren't good fits for your business. Constant boundary violations, unreasonable deadline demands, abusive communication, consistent late payments, or scope creep that never stops signal problematic relationships.

Some clients are just bad matches for your working style rather than difficult. Clients who need constant reassurance might not work well with your direct communication style. Clients who want daily check-ins might conflict with your deep-work preferences.

Document problem behaviors and your responses to build a case for termination. Track missed payments, scope creep requests, boundary violations, and abusive communications. This documentation protects you if the client relationship ends badly.

Address problems before moving to termination. Sometimes clients don't realize their behavior is problematic. Clear communication about expectations and consequences can resolve issues without ending the relationship.

"Our agreement specifies a 48-hour turnaround for feedback. When feedback is delayed, it pushes back all subsequent deadlines and affects other client projects. Going forward, we'll need to adjust project timelines to account for feedback delays."

Calculate the true cost of problematic clients including time spent managing drama, opportunity cost of turning down good clients, stress impact on your health, and damage to work quality for other clients. Problem clients often cost more than their revenue justifies.

Plan client termination carefully to protect your reputation and business relationships. Finish current projects professionally, provide transition support where appropriate, and maintain courteous communication even when ending the relationship.

Use neutral, professional language when terminating client relationships. "We've determined that our working styles aren't aligned for future projects" avoids blame while clearly ending the relationship.

Have backup plans for replacing difficult client revenue before firing them. Ending client relationships is easier when you're not desperate for their income. Build your client pipeline so you can afford to be selective.

Create termination policies before you need them. Having standard procedures for ending client relationships removes emotion from difficult decisions and ensures you handle terminations professionally.

Refer problem clients to other providers when possible. This maintains goodwill while getting them out of your business. Some clients who don't work with your style might be perfect for other service providers.

Learn from each client termination to improve your client selection process. What warning signs did you miss during the sales process? What questions could have identified the mismatch earlier? Use this information to screen future prospects better.

Career Moves

Career advancement for neurodivergent marketers doesn't follow the traditional path. Your scattered interests might create a portfolio that looks unfocused to neurotypical hiring managers. Your communication style might not shine in standard interview formats. Your need for accommodations might make you hesitant to pursue opportunities that seem inflexible.

But your unique perspective, deep expertise in your areas of interest, and systematic thinking are valuable assets that the right employers need. The key is learning to position these strengths effectively and finding career paths that work with your neurodivergent traits rather than against them.

I never had imposter syndrome in the traditional sense. I always knew what I was doing. What changed over time wasn't confidence — it was calibration. Some periods I knew I was operating at a high level. Other periods I knew I was at a lower level and why. That self-awareness is more useful than either false confidence or manufactured doubt. Know where you are on the scale and adjust accordingly.

Interview Strategies That Work

Traditional interview advice assumes you can think on your feet, read social cues easily, and sell yourself confidently in real-time conversations. For neurodivergent brains, this approach often leads to poor performance that doesn't reflect your capabilities.

Prepare extensively but focus on frameworks rather than memorizing answers. Research the company, understand their challenges, and develop 3-4 key stories that demonstrate your value. These stories should show problem-solving skills, results achieved, and how you work with teams.

Create a "story bank" that includes: a time you solved a complex problem systematically, a project where your attention to detail prevented major issues, a situation where your research uncovered insights others missed, and an example of how you improved processes or systems.

Practice telling these stories concisely but don't script them word-for-word. You want natural delivery that adapts to different questions, not robotic recitation of memorized responses.

Request information about interview format in advance. Will it be behavioral questions, technical discussions, or case study problems? Knowing the structure helps you prepare appropriately and reduces anxiety about unknown expectations.

Ask for accommodations that help you perform your best. This might include written questions in advance, extra time to process complex scenarios, or the ability to take notes during the interview. Frame these requests as helping you demonstrate your capabilities clearly.

Use your systematic thinking as an interview advantage. When asked about challenges or problems, walk through your analytical process step by step. Show how you gather information, evaluate options, and make decisions. This demonstrates valuable problem-solving skills.

Prepare thoughtful questions that show your analytical thinking. Ask about the company's biggest marketing challenges, how they measure success, what tools and processes they use, and how the team collaborates. These questions demonstrate genuine interest and strategic thinking.

Practice discussing your neurodivergent traits as professional strengths when relevant. Your ADHD hyperfocus becomes "ability to dive deep into complex research." Your autistic attention to detail becomes "systematic approach to quality control." Your introversion becomes "thoughtful analysis and preparation."

Follow up after interviews with additional information or examples that reinforce your capabilities. If you thought of a better answer to a question, or if you have relevant work samples that relate to their challenges, send a thoughtful follow-up email.

Portfolio Building for Scattered Careers

Neurodivergent marketers often have diverse career paths that reflect their varied interests and natural tendency to explore different specialties deeply. This diversity can look scattered to employers who expect linear career progression, but it's a significant advantage when positioned properly.

Organize your portfolio around capabilities rather than chronological experience. Group your work into categories like "data analysis and optimization," "content strategy and creation," "campaign development and management," and "process improvement and automation."

This approach lets you show expertise depth while explaining why you've worked across different industries or roles. Your scattered experience becomes evidence of versatility and learning ability rather than lack of focus.

Create case studies that demonstrate your systematic thinking and results orientation. Don't just show the final deliverables; explain the problems you solved, your analytical process, and the business impact of your work.

A good case study includes: the challenge or problem, your research and analysis approach, the solutions you developed, how you implemented them, and the measurable results achieved. This format shows both your thinking process and your ability to drive outcomes.

Highlight work that demonstrates your neurodivergent strengths. Projects where your research obsession uncovered insights, campaigns where your attention to detail prevented costly mistakes, or processes where your systematic thinking improved efficiency.

Include work that shows you can collaborate effectively despite any social challenges. Team projects, client relationships, and cross-functional initiatives demonstrate that your working style produces results in professional environments.

Document your learning and adaptation abilities. Show how you've mastered new tools, adapted to different industries, or developed expertise in emerging areas. This positions career diversity as curiosity and growth orientation rather than inability to commit.

Create different portfolio versions for different types of opportunities. Emphasize analytical work for data-focused roles, creative projects for content positions, or systematic process improvements for operations roles. Tailor your presentation to match what each employer values most.

Use your portfolio to address potential concerns proactively. If your career path includes short stints at multiple companies, explain how each role built skills or expertise. If you've changed industries frequently, show how core marketing principles apply across different contexts.

Freelance vs Agency vs In-House

Each career path has advantages and challenges for neurodivergent marketers. The best choice depends on your traits, life circumstances, and career goals. Understanding the trade-offs helps you make decisions that support your long-term success and wellbeing.

Freelancing offers maximum flexibility and control over your working environment. You can set your own schedule, choose your clients, and design processes that work with your neurodivergent traits. You're not subject to office politics or social expectations that drain your energy.

The challenges include irregular income, administrative responsibilities, and the need to handle client acquisition and business development. You also miss out on team collaboration, structured learning opportunities, and employer-provided benefits.

Freelancing works well if you're self-motivated, comfortable with financial uncertainty, and prefer working independently. It's also good if you need accommodations that traditional employers might resist providing.

Agency work provides variety, fast-paced learning, and exposure to different industries and challenges. You'll work with diverse clients and have opportunities to develop expertise across multiple marketing disciplines. Agencies often have sophisticated tools and resources that enhance your capabilities.

The downsides include high-pressure environments, frequent context switching, and competitive cultures that might not accommodate neurodivergent working styles. Agency environments can be overstimulating and may not provide the consistency that helps some neurodivergent people thrive.

Agency work suits neurodivergent marketers who thrive on variety, learn quickly, and can handle fast-paced environments. It's less suitable if you need quiet work environments, struggle with frequent interruptions, or require extensive time to process new information.

In-house roles offer stability, deeper relationships with colleagues, and the opportunity to develop long-term expertise in industries or business models. You can build systems and processes that compound over time rather than starting fresh with each client.

The trade-offs include slower career advancement, limited exposure to different approaches, and office politics that might be challenging to navigate. You may also have less control over your work environment and processes.

In-house positions work well for neurodivergent marketers who prefer consistency, enjoy building deep expertise, and work well within established systems. They're less suitable if you need constant variety or struggle with traditional corporate environments.

Consider hybrid approaches that combine benefits from different paths. You might work in-house part-time while building a freelance practice, consult for agencies on projects, or move between different types of roles as your career evolves.

The key is choosing career paths that align with your neurodivergent traits rather than fighting against them. Your ideal career might look different from traditional progression paths, but it should use your strengths and support your long-term success and wellbeing.

Career advancement for neurodivergent marketers requires strategic thinking about how to position your unique capabilities and find environments where those capabilities are valued. Success comes from knowing your strengths and finding career paths that let you use them effectively.

Freelancing for Neurodivergents

Freelancing can be perfect for neurodivergent marketers or terrible, depending on how you structure your business. The freedom to work on your own schedule, choose your clients, and design your environment sounds ideal. But the chaos of inconsistent income, constant client acquisition, and administrative overwhelm can trigger every executive function challenge you have.

The key is building freelance systems that use your neurodivergent strengths while protecting you from the aspects of self-employment that could destroy your productivity and mental health.

Your systematic thinking can create predictable business processes. Your attention to detail can produce quality that commands premium pricing. Your deep focus abilities can deliver results that generate referrals and repeat business.

Client Acquisition That Doesn't Suck

Traditional freelance advice tells you to network constantly, pitch everyone, and hustle until you make it. This approach burns out neurodivergent freelancers who can't maintain the social energy required for endless business development activities.

Build client acquisition systems that work with your energy patterns instead of requiring constant networking and sales activities. Focus on methods that use your expertise and systematic thinking rather than your social skills.

Create valuable content that attracts ideal clients instead of chasing prospects who might not be interested.

Blog posts, case studies, guides, and educational resources demonstrate your expertise while drawing people to you rather than requiring you to find them.

I generate most of my leads through detailed case studies that show my systematic approach to marketing problems. Potential clients find these through search engines when they're researching solutions, then contact me understanding my methods and value.

Develop referral systems that turn satisfied clients into ongoing lead sources. Create processes for requesting referrals, staying in touch with past clients, and making it easy for people to recommend your services to others.

Use your systematic thinking to optimize one or two lead generation methods rather than trying every marketing tactic. Master content marketing or LinkedIn outreach or speaking at industry events, then systematically improve your results over time.

Build partnerships with complementary service providers who work with your ideal clients. Web designers, business coaches, and other marketers can become referral sources when you create mutually beneficial relationships.

Position yourself as a specialist rather than a generalist to reduce competition and increase pricing power. Being the go-to expert for email marketing automation or B2B content strategy makes you easier to find and harder to replace.

Track your client acquisition metrics to understand what's working and optimize your efforts accordingly. Monitor which lead sources produce the best clients, what conversion rates you achieve, and how long sales cycles take.

Create standardized sales processes that reduce the energy drain of client acquisition. Templates for proposals, discovery calls, and contracts help you maintain quality while reducing the mental effort required for each prospect.

Pricing for Your Value

Neurodivergent freelancers often underprice their services because they focus on time investment rather than value delivery. Your systematic approach, attention to detail, and deep expertise create more value than generic marketing services, but you need to price accordingly.

Stop pricing based on hours and start pricing based on outcomes and value delivered. Clients care about results, not how long you spend producing them. Your efficiency should increase your profits, not decrease your rates.

Research market rates for your specialty and position yourself in the premium tier. Your systematic approach and quality standards justify higher pricing than average providers. Don't compete on price with marketers who deliver sloppy work.

Create package-based pricing that reflects the full scope of your systematic approach. Instead of charging hourly for campaign development, create packages that include research, strategy development, implementation, and optimization.

My email marketing packages include deliverability audit, list segmentation strategy, automation workflow design, template creation, and 90-day optimization support. This systematic approach delivers more value than hourly consulting.

Build value-based pricing around business outcomes rather than activities. Price based on the revenue generated, costs saved, or efficiency improved rather than the time required to achieve those results.

Use your perfectionist tendencies as pricing justification. The quality, thoroughness, and attention to detail that your neurodivergent traits provide are valuable differentiators that support premium pricing.

Document case studies that demonstrate the ROI of your systematic approach. Show how your attention to detail prevented costly mistakes, how your research uncovered valuable insights, or how your optimization improved results over time.

Create pricing tiers that give clients options while protecting your profitability. Basic packages provide core services, premium packages include additional analysis and optimization, and enterprise packages offer comprehensive strategic support.

Raise your rates regularly to reflect your growing expertise and the increasing value you provide. Your systematic approach to skill development means you're constantly becoming more valuable to clients.

Administrative Systems That Run Themselves

Administrative tasks are the enemy of neurodivergent productivity. Invoicing, project tracking, client communication, and business development can consume the mental energy you need for marketing work. The solution is automating everything possible and systematizing the rest.

Set up automated systems for routine business processes that don't require creative thinking. Invoice generation, payment processing, project status updates, and follow-up sequences can run automatically with minimal ongoing attention.

Use project management tools that track progress and communicate status without requiring constant manual updates. Tools like Asana, Trello, or Monday can automate notifications, deadline reminders, and progress reports.

Create template libraries for all routine communications. Email responses, project proposals, status updates, and contract terms should be standardized to reduce decision fatigue and ensure consistent quality.

I have templates for: initial client inquiry responses, discovery call follow-ups, proposal submissions, project kickoff emails, weekly status updates, project completion summaries, and invoice delivery messages. This covers 90% of my client communication without requiring original writing.

Automate financial tracking and reporting to reduce bookkeeping overhead. Tools like QuickBooks, FreshBooks, or Wave can categorize expenses, track income, and generate reports automatically.

Build client onboarding systems that gather necessary information systematically while creating professional first impressions. Automated welcome sequences, information-gathering forms, and project setup checklists ensure nothing gets missed.

Use scheduling tools to eliminate the back-and-forth of meeting coordination. Calendly, Acuity, or similar tools let clients book time while respecting your availability preferences and energy management needs.

Create systematic approaches to project delivery that ensure consistent quality without requiring perfect memory. Checklists, templates, and standard procedures help you deliver professional results even when executive function is struggling.

Set up automated backup and file organization systems to protect your work and make information easy to find. Cloud storage with automatic syncing and organized folder structures prevent lost work and reduce stress.

Build regular review processes into your business operations to identify optimization opportunities and prevent small problems from becoming large issues. Monthly business reviews, quarterly pricing evaluations, and annual process audits keep your systems running smoothly.

Agency Life Survival

Agency environments can be either perfect training grounds for neurodivergent marketers or overwhelming chaos machines that burn you out within months. The fast pace, diverse projects, and collaborative culture offer learning opportunities you can't get elsewhere. But the constant interruptions, unclear priorities, and high-pressure deadlines can trigger every executive function challenge you have.

Success in agency life requires choosing the right environment and developing strategies that let you thrive within agency culture without sacrificing your mental health or working style.

Your systematic thinking can bring order to chaotic projects. Your attention to detail can catch expensive mistakes before they reach clients. Your deep focus abilities can produce work when you learn to protect your concentration in busy environments.

Choosing the Right Agency

Not all agencies are created equal for neurodivergent professionals. Some cultures embrace systematic thinking and quality focus. Others reward whoever can speak loudest in meetings and handle constant interruptions. Choosing wisely makes the difference between career growth and burnout.

Research agency culture before applying, not just their client list and creative work. Look for signs of how they handle different working styles, what their communication norms are, and whether they value systematic approaches or just creative brainstorming.

The worst agencies I encountered had one thing in common: they weren't tracking anything meaningful. No real statistics on what was working, no accountability to numbers. Everything ran on gut feelings and whoever talked loudest in the room. When you don't manage with data, you don't improve — you just repeat the same mistakes with more confidence.

Read employee reviews on sites like Glassdoor, but focus on comments about work-life balance, management style, and whether people feel supported. Generic complaints about "long hours" matter less than comments about micromanagement or lack of process.

During interviews, ask about typical workdays, collaboration styles, and how they handle different personality types. "How do you support employees who work best with minimal interruptions?" reveals more than "What's the culture like?"

Look for agencies that have documented processes and systematic approaches to client work. Agencies that wing everything are harder environments for neurodivergent professionals who thrive with structure and predictability.

Consider smaller agencies or boutiques that might offer more flexibility than large traditional agencies. Smaller teams often allow for more accommodation of different working styles and may appreciate your systematic approach more.

Pay attention to physical workspace design during interviews. Open floor plans with constant noise and interruptions are challenging for many neurodivergent people. Agencies with quiet work areas or flexible seating arrangements might be better fits.

Ask about remote work policies and flexible scheduling. Agencies that allow work-from-home days or flexible hours give you more control over your environment and energy management.

Evaluate the types of clients and projects the agency handles. Fast-moving consumer brands with constant campaign changes might be overwhelming, while B2B clients with longer planning cycles might suit your working style better.

Look for agencies that value specialization alongside collaboration. Places where you can develop deep expertise in areas while contributing to team projects offer the best of both worlds.

Managing Agency Chaos

Agency environments are chaotic. Client priorities change suddenly. New projects appear with impossible deadlines. Team members get pulled onto urgent tasks mid-project. Learning to navigate this chaos without losing your productivity or sanity is essential for agency success.

Create personal organization systems that work independently of agency chaos. Your project tracking, priority management, and deadline monitoring can't depend on agency systems that might change or break under pressure.

I use a personal task management system that mirrors agency project management but gives me more control. I track my own deadlines, document decisions that affect my work, and maintain my own project status regardless of what's happening in agency systems.

Build relationships with colleagues who can help you navigate social dynamics and unclear communication. Find allies who can translate ambiguous feedback, explain unwritten rules, and provide heads-up about changes that might affect your work.

Develop rapid context-switching strategies that let you move between projects without losing focus. This might include transition rituals, project summary sheets, or physical cues that help your brain shift gears quickly.

Learn to distinguish between urgent requests and manufactured urgency that comes from poor planning. Not every "rush" project requires dropping everything else. Develop skills for negotiating priorities and managing competing demands.

Create boundaries around your most productive work time while remaining flexible for true emergencies. Protect your peak focus hours for complex work while remaining available for collaboration during other times.

Document everything because agency environments often have poor institutional memory. Keep records of project requirements, client feedback, and decisions so you can reference them when priorities shift or team members change.

Use your systematic thinking to identify patterns in agency chaos and develop strategies for common scenarios. If certain types of projects always have last-minute changes, build extra buffer time. If clients always request revisions, plan accordingly.

Moving Up Without Burning Out

Agency career advancement often rewards people who can handle endless multitasking, work long hours consistently, and thrive on constant social interaction. This advancement model can be challenging for neurodivergent professionals, but alternative paths exist.

Focus on developing deep expertise that makes you valuable rather than trying to be the loudest voice in every meeting. Agencies need people who can solve complex problems, not just manage multiple projects simultaneously.

Become the go-to person for types of work that match your strengths. Being the agency's expert in marketing automation, data analysis, or quality assurance can lead to advancement without requiring traditional management skills.

My career advancement came from becoming the agency's specialist in email marketing and marketing automation. Clients requested me by name for these projects, which created advancement opportunities based on expertise rather than general management ability.

Document your contributions and results systematically to make your value visible during review periods. Agencies often overlook systematic contributors in favor of more vocal self-promoters, so you need clear evidence of your impact.

Seek out projects that showcase your systematic thinking and quality focus. Volunteer for complex analyses, process improvement initiatives, or quality control roles that demonstrate your unique value.

Build relationships with clients who appreciate your working style. Client relationships can drive internal advancement when clients request your involvement in their projects.

Consider advancement paths that don't require managing large teams. Senior specialist roles, client relationship management, or strategic consulting positions might fit your skills better than traditional account management.

Negotiate for the accommodations and working conditions you need as you advance. Higher-level positions often come with more control over your schedule and working environment.

Set clear boundaries around work hours and availability to prevent the burnout that destroys many agency careers. Sustainable high performance beats unsustainable heroics every time.

Look for mentorship from senior professionals who understand different working styles. The best mentors help you advance in ways that work with your neurodivergent traits rather than fighting against them.

Consider whether long-term agency employment fits your career goals or if agencies should be stepping stones to other opportunities. Some neurodivergent professionals thrive in agency environments, while others use agency experience to build skills for consulting or in-house roles.

In-House Marketing

In-house marketing roles offer stability, deep industry knowledge, and the chance to build long-term strategies without constantly acquiring new clients. For neurodivergent marketers, in-house positions can provide the consistency and relationship depth that make work more manageable and rewarding.

But corporate environments also bring unique challenges. Office politics, unclear decision-making processes, and competing priorities can overwhelm neurodivergent professionals who thrive on structure and clear communication. Success requires learning to navigate corporate systems while building the internal relationships and processes that support your work.

Your systematic thinking can improve marketing operations that have grown chaotic over time. Your attention to detail can catch compliance issues and quality problems that cost companies money. Your ability to focus deeply can produce strategic insights that drive business growth.

Corporate Navigation

Corporate environments have unwritten rules, informal power structures, and cultural norms that aren't obvious to neurodivergent professionals. Learning to read these systems and work within them is essential for in-house marketing success.

Map the informal decision-making processes in your organization, not just the official org chart. Understanding who influences decisions, who needs to be consulted, and who can derail projects helps you navigate corporate politics more effectively.

I discovered that our CMO always checked with the CFO before approving budget requests, even though this wasn't documented anywhere. Building that step into my approval process prevented delays and improved my success rate with funding requests.

Identify key stakeholders who can support your marketing initiatives and invest time in building relationships with them. Sales leaders, product managers, customer service teams, and executives all have different perspectives that can help or hinder your work.

Learn the communication preferences of different leaders and adapt your approach accordingly. Some executives prefer detailed data analysis. Others want high-level summaries. Some like face-to-face meetings. Others prefer written updates.

Document corporate processes and decision criteria to reduce uncertainty and improve your planning. Understanding budget cycles, approval requirements, and project timelines helps you work more effectively within corporate constraints.

Build alliances with colleagues who can help you understand corporate culture and navigate complex situations. Find mentors or allies who can explain unwritten rules and provide guidance when you're unsure about appropriate responses.

Participate in corporate initiatives and committees when they align with your expertise and interests. This visibility can build your reputation while contributing to areas where your systematic thinking adds value.

Learn to frame your marketing proposals in language that resonates with corporate priorities. Instead of talking about creative campaigns, discuss ROI, efficiency improvements, and competitive advantages that matter to business leaders.

Building Internal Systems

Many companies have marketing operations that grew organically without systematic design. Your ability to create order from chaos can improve marketing effectiveness while advancing your career.

Audit existing marketing processes to identify inefficiencies, gaps, and opportunities for improvement. Your attention to detail and systematic thinking can uncover problems that others have learned to work around.

Create documentation for marketing processes that exist only in people's heads. When key team members leave or get promoted, institutional knowledge disappears unless it's captured systematically.

My first major contribution was documenting our lead qualification process, which had never been written down. Sales and marketing were using different criteria, causing confusion and missed opportunities. Clear documentation improved conversion rates and team collaboration.

Build marketing technology stacks that integrate properly and provide the data visibility you need for optimization. Many companies have disconnected tools that create data silos and manual workarounds.

Develop standard operating procedures for routine marketing activities like campaign development, content creation, and performance reporting. Standardization improves quality while reducing the mental energy required for routine tasks.

Create measurement frameworks that track the metrics that matter to business outcomes, not just marketing vanity metrics. Your analytical skills can help companies understand which marketing activities drive real business results.

Implement quality control processes that catch errors before they reach customers or damage brand reputation. Your perfectionist tendencies become valuable business assets when applied to brand consistency and compliance.

Build cross-functional workflows that improve collaboration between marketing and other departments. Understanding how marketing impacts sales, customer service, and product development helps you create more effective integrated strategies.

Stakeholder Management

In-house marketers serve multiple internal stakeholders with different priorities, timelines, and success metrics. Managing these relationships while maintaining your sanity requires systematic approaches to communication and expectation setting.

Identify the key stakeholders for each marketing initiative and understand their interests and concerns. Sales teams care about lead quality. Product teams care about feature adoption. Executives care about revenue impact.

Create regular communication rhythms that keep stakeholders informed without overwhelming them with unnecessary details. Weekly status updates, monthly performance reviews, and quarterly strategic discussions provide structure for ongoing relationships.

Use your systematic thinking to anticipate stakeholder needs and address concerns before they become problems. If you know the sales team always asks about lead volume, include that data in your standard reports.

Develop stakeholder communication materials that speak to their priorities and expertise levels. Technical teams might want detailed implementation plans while executives prefer high-level strategic summaries.

Build consensus systematically rather than hoping stakeholders will align. Document requirements, facilitate discussions about trade-offs, and create shared understanding of priorities and constraints.

Learn to say no strategically when stakeholder requests conflict with marketing priorities or available resources. Frame declining requests in terms of impact on agreed-upon goals rather than personal preferences.

Create feedback loops that help you understand how your marketing work affects other departments. Regular check-ins with sales, customer service, and product teams provide insights that improve your strategic planning.

Manage up effectively by keeping your manager and senior leadership informed about marketing progress, challenges, and resource needs. Your systematic approach to documentation and analysis can make these conversations more productive.

Track stakeholder satisfaction alongside marketing performance metrics. Internal customer satisfaction affects your ability to get resources, support, and cooperation for future initiatives.

Use your attention to detail to deliver on commitments consistently. Reliable execution builds trust with stakeholders who may have been disappointed by previous marketing teams.

Essential Tools

There is a version of tool evaluation that is productive and a version that is procrastination. The productive version takes a few hours, picks something good enough, and gets back to work. The other version becomes a months-long research project while your lead pipeline sits empty. Every hour you spend comparing project management platforms is an hour you didn't spend finding a client. Be honest with yourself about which one you're doing.

You don't need many tools. You need a few that you'll actually use consistently. Here's what my stack actually looks like: Claude for rough drafts, my calendar for scheduling, and a paper grid for project tracking. LinkedIn and Facebook for finding prospects and staying visible. That's most of it. The rest depends on the specific work.

Project Management That Helps

The best project management tool is the one you'll actually use. For me that's paper. A grid where I log what I've done as I do it, not a system I have to update and maintain and remember to check. Every CRM and task manager I've tried required more energy to maintain than it saved. Yours might be different. The point is to find out through actual use, not through reading comparison articles.

If you need something digital, keep it simple. A tool with fifty features you'll never use creates cognitive overhead, not efficiency. Todoist, a plain calendar, or even a well-organized spreadsheet will outperform an elaborate system you never fully set up.

Whatever you choose: use your calendar as the backbone. Everything that has a deadline or a time goes on the calendar. Not in a separate app you might check, not in your head — on the calendar. That one habit will do more for your productivity than any project management platform.

Content Tools That Save Time

For writing, I start with Claude to get a rough draft on the page, then rewrite it in my own voice. The AI handles the blank page problem. I handle making it sound like me. That combination works well for the way my brain operates — I'm a better editor than I am a starter.

For design, Canva covers most needs without requiring you to learn a professional tool. For scheduling, Buffer or Hootsuite handle the mechanics of getting content out consistently. Neither requires significant setup time or ongoing maintenance.

One warning on automation tools for social media: be careful. LinkedIn and Facebook will kill accounts they detect are using automation to post or engage. The platforms want human activity, and they've gotten good at detecting when it isn't. Use scheduling tools for posting times — that's generally fine. Use bots to auto-connect, auto-comment, or auto-message — that's how you lose the account.

Build a content library of things you've already created: past posts that performed well, testimonials, case study snapshots, behind-the-scenes material. Evergreen content you can reshare during low-energy periods reduces the pressure to create something new every time you need to post.

Analytics Without Overwhelm

Track what connects to income. Website traffic growth, email list growth, conversion rate, revenue per subscriber. Those four numbers tell you whether your marketing is working. Everything else is context at best and distraction at worst.

The platforms provide more data than you could ever meaningfully use. Ignore most of it. Start with the pre-built dashboards in Google Analytics, your email platform, and whatever social channels you're using. Don't build custom reports until you've outgrown the defaults — most people never do.

Check metrics on a schedule, not compulsively. Weekly is enough for most things. Set up alerts for significant changes so you don't have to monitor constantly. The goal is catching problems and spotting patterns — not watching numbers all day.

When you see a spike or a drop, note what you were doing at the time. That correlation builds into real knowledge over months. The marketer who knows what actually moved their numbers has a permanent advantage over the one pulling reports without context.

Your Personal System

Every system in this book is a starting point, not a prescription. The one that works is the one built around your brain, your business model, and your actual life — not someone else's version of what a productive marketer looks like.

My daily system is simple by design. Comment on a dozen LinkedIn and Facebook posts each morning. Respond to any comments that warrant a response. Send a few direct messages to people I want to stay connected with. Three times a week, write a post — text with a graphic, no video, no elaborate production. Once a week, run a poll. That's the engine. It's repeatable, it fits my energy patterns, and it doesn't require me to be someone I'm not.

I don't need a massive lead pipeline. My business model doesn't require it. That's a point most marketing advice completely ignores: the right system depends on what you're selling and how many clients you can actually serve. Build for your reality, not for the version of success someone is selling in a webinar.

Building Your Methodology

Start by being honest about how your brain actually works, not how you wish it worked. If you hyperfocus, build your system around capturing that energy when it arrives. If you need structure, build in checkpoints. If you run out of steam by 2 PM, don't schedule your most important work for 3 PM. The system has to fit the brain running it.

Then look at your business model. How many clients do you need? How do they find you? What does a typical week of work actually look like? Your marketing system exists to feed that — not to look impressive, not to follow best practices, not to do what someone at a conference told you to do.

Build the minimum viable version first. The simplest set of activities that keeps you visible and generates the leads you need. Do that consistently for ninety days before you add anything. Most people never get to consistent — they keep adding complexity instead of executing the basics.

One warning that will save you significant time and money: avoid webinars. Almost all of them are sales funnels dressed up as education. LinkedIn events are the same. If you genuinely need training on something, get it from Udemy or a similar platform — paid courses without ads, without upsells, without someone trying to sell you a mastermind at the end. Pay for the knowledge, skip the pitch.

Documentation That Helps

Document what works while you're doing it, not afterward. A simple running note during a project captures the decisions you made and why. That's the documentation that's actually useful — not a comprehensive system you built on a Sunday afternoon and never touched again.

The things worth documenting: your client onboarding steps, your content creation process, your quality checklist before anything goes out. The things not worth documenting: everything else until you've done it enough times that the friction is actually costing you something.

Keep documentation in the simplest format you'll actually maintain. A text file, a single spreadsheet, a notes app. Elaborate documentation systems are another form of procrastination. If you're spending more time documenting your process than doing it, something has gone wrong.

Continuous Improvement Without Obsessing

Review what's working once a month. Not daily, not weekly — monthly. Ask three questions: What produced results? What wasted time? What should change? Make one or two adjustments and move on. The perfectionist tendency is to turn the review into a complete system overhaul. Don't. Small consistent improvements compound. Complete rebuilds just restart the clock.

The goal is a system you can run without thinking too hard about it. When your marketing activities become habits — things you do because that's just what Tuesday looks like — you've built something real. Until then, you're still experimenting. Both are fine. Just know which one you're doing.

Build it around your brain. Run it consistently. Kill what doesn't work. That's the whole system.

Conclusion

Here's the most important thing I can tell you, and I'm going to say it directly because you've earned a straight answer by getting to the end of this book:

Stop listening to other people.

ADHD brains have a particular vulnerability to authority figures. We find someone who seems to have figured it out, and we latch on. We follow their system, buy their courses, attend their events, join their masterminds. We stay way too long and spend way too much money trying to make their approach work for a brain that was never the one they were talking to.

I did this. Repeatedly. It cost me time and money I didn't have to spare, and the worst part is that none of it was necessary. The answers I needed came from experimenting with my own business, not from following someone else's blueprint.

What Comes Next

If you need to learn something, learn it cheaply first. Udemy runs sales constantly — wait for one and pay ten dollars for a course instead of a thousand dollars for a program. Get the knowledge without the pitch, without the upsell, without the six-week live cohort designed to keep you dependent on the teacher.

Then experiment. Small. Cheap. Low stakes. Run the thing, see what happens, adjust. Don't spend significant money on anything until you've tested the concept with your own audience in your own market and seen it work with your own eyes. Other people's results are not evidence that something will work for you. Your results are.

This is especially important for neurodivergent marketers because we tend to research obsessively, become convinced something will work, and then go all in before we've tested anything. The research feels like action. It isn't. The experiment is the action. Start there.

Your Competitive Advantage

The marketing industry is full of people running someone else's system. They attended the same webinars, bought the same courses, follow the same gurus, and produce roughly the same results as everyone else in that world.

Your neurodivergent brain, used correctly, is a way out of that sameness. Your hyperfocus produces depth that surface-level competitors can't match. Your pattern recognition spots opportunities others miss. Your systematic thinking builds processes that actually hold up over time. Your perfectionism catches the errors that cost other people clients and money.

These aren't consolation prizes for having a difficult brain. They're real advantages in a field that desperately needs people who can think carefully, work systematically, and deliver consistent quality. The market rewards those things. You have them.

The Path Forward

Build a system that fits your brain. Test everything before you spend on it. Ignore authority figures who want you to stay in their orbit. Learn from courses that don't have an agenda beyond teaching you the thing.

Most importantly: trust what you discover through your own experimentation more than anything you read, including this book. I've told you what worked for me. Your job is to find out what works for you.

Now go find out.

Books by Richard Lowe

See books by Richard Lowe at
https://masterofworlds.com

Get free publishing insights and industry updates at
https://thewritingking.substack.com

For ghostwriting and book coaching services see
https://thewritingking.com